Ten on Tin

MY MCKINLEY STREET YEARS
1950–1960

A Coming of Age on Tinbridge Hill

DUBOIS MILLER

©2011 by DuBois Miller

Published 2011

First edition

ISBN: 978-0-9830-482-8-2
Library of Congress Control Number: 2011937842
Printed in the United States of America
Published by Blackwell Press, Lynchburg, Virginia

BLACKWELL
PRESS

Blackwell Press
311 Rivermont Avenue
Lynchburg, Virginia 24504
434-528-4665
www.BlackwellPress.net

Contents

Acknowledgements iii

Introduction v

Polk Street Beginnings 1

This Old House 7

Technology Makeover 11

A Fuel's Errand 17

The Terrain of My Domain 21

New Friends and Neighbors 35

Dog Eat Dog and Other Animals 45

Accidents Do Happen 55

Fruit of the Limbs 61

Oh, Blackwater and Tunnel Vision 65

Pool Days 75

Hot Wheels 85

Fun and Games 91

Up in Smoke 103

Race and Other Relations 111

Crime and Punishment 123

Smackdowns 131

School of Soft Knocks 135

The Sound of Music 155

Final Days 161

Epilogue 165

About the Author 169

Index 171

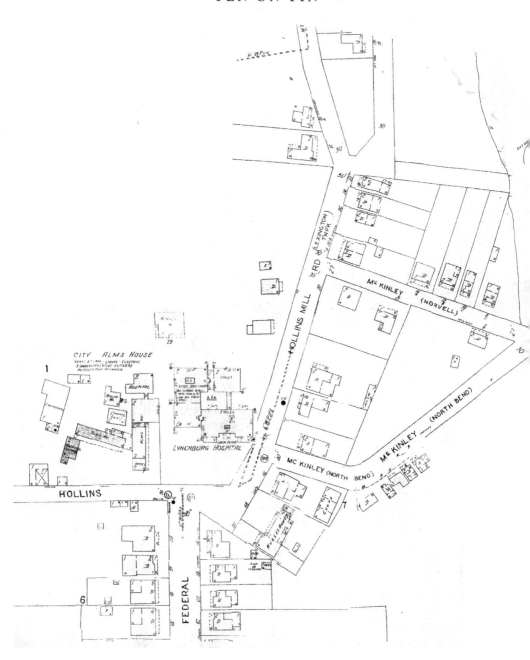

1927 Sanborn map of the McKinley Street area.
Courtesy of Nancy Marion

ii

Acknowledgements

Anything I have written has been done with the admission that being an author is outside of my range of expertise. For most of my life I have sought to remain in the shadows of real luminaries. Now retired, I would like to shed some light on my early life as a contribution to the history of my hometown of Lynchburg, Virginia.

This book is written for the citizens of Lynchburg and dedicated to my friends and neighbors of Tinbridge Hill. Although I wrote this book using limited resources, it could not have been written without contributions from people from my past and present. I owe a great deal to Carolyn Bell, who edited my manuscript, gave me sound advice, and inspired me to broaden my vision.

Since my recollection of events may differ from others', I have tried, when possible, to get input from family, friends, and former neighbors. My sister, Wilhelminia, and my brother, Lafayette, were my first sources of information. Others who provided me with some of the details of this book were my friends Hilda Rucker Adams, Randolph Austin, Lillian Austin Jones, Clifford Fox, Elaine Johnson, Mary Johnson Woodruff, George Rucker, Robert Rucker, and Steve Rucker. If, by mental displacement, inaccuracies

My Aunt Julia bought this Kodak camera for my mother and the same camera for herself.

iii

appear in the details of this book, I apologize for my faulty memory.

I would like to thank my late aunt, Julia Bolling, who saved the photographs she took of my family, friends, and pets.

A special thank-you goes to Nancy Marion, and Grafton Blankinship who gave me access to their resources and expertise.

It is my sincere hope that this book will paint a picture of life in Lynchburg that adds to the history and culture of the city I have come to appreciate on so many levels.

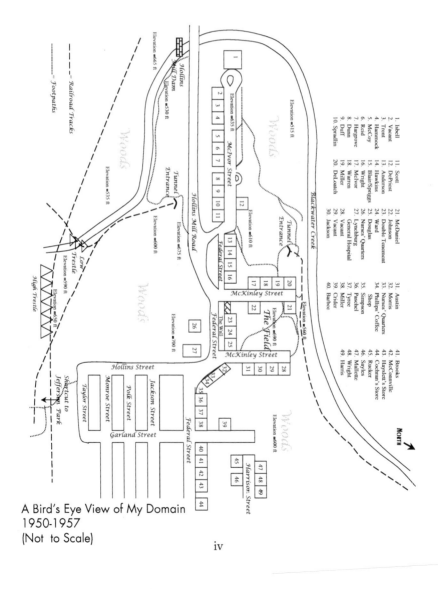

A Bird's Eye View of My Domain
1950-1957
(Not to Scale)

Introduction

Before Carolyn Bell, one of the founding board members of the Legacy Museum of African American History, asked me to participate in a project capturing the history of Tinbridge Hill, I had taken writing off my bucket list. Carolyn wanted me to submit a five-page essay about growing up in this neighborhood. While piecing together my contribution, I convinced myself that other residents of Lynchburg could benefit if I broadened my essay. Consequently, I expanded my writing project to book form, thereby giving myself a greater literary challenge and an opportunity to add to the legacy of my community.

In as humble and entertaining a way as my limited writing skills will allow, I have created an account of my life on Tinbridge Hill, concentrating on the ten years spent living on McKinley Street; hence the title: *Ten on Tin*.

My brother, Lafayette, and I agree that these were some of the best years of our lives. More so for me, because I spent key formative years, from ages five to fifteen, in what I think of as the best of two worlds: that of an urban dweller and that of a junior naturalist.

I realize that much of how and what I remember is based on my current feelings, which have developed from maturity and reflection. But both maturity and reflection have been hardwired with the experiences of my youth.

Throughout this book, I use "we" and "us" to refer to any combination of boys with whom I grew up. Counted among my childhood friendships are Henry "Junie" Scott, William "Bill" McDaniel, Paul Simon, Jr., Mitchell McCoy, and Randolph Austin. This was my core group of friends while I lived on McKinley Street.

If I have put my words together with clarity and without straying too far off course, then you may find both enlightenment and humor in my memories of a neighborhood that time has forgotten.

Clockwise from top left: My mother, Frances Miller; father, Carl Miller, Sr.; my aunt, Julia Bolling; siblings (l to r) Carl, Jr., Wilhelminia, and Lafayette; me at age seven.

Polk Street Beginnings

I have no memories of my life on Polk Street until my family moved from 62 Polk, where I was born in 1944, to 76 Polk, where I became quite aware of my surroundings.

My parents and older siblings moved to Jackson Street, about two blocks from my first home at 62 Polk, from Bedford County —a migration pattern of many rural blacks in economic poverty in the 1940s. Our nuclear family included my

Carl, Jr., and Lafayette sit on a 1936 Buick Super 8.

mother, my father (who was more like an electron, orbiting our center, while working in Washington, DC), my oldest brother, Carl, Jr. ("Noon"), my brother Lafayette ("Cutchie"), and my sister, Wilhelminia ("Billie").

Momma dubbed me Maynor DuBois Miller after a round of debates with elders, who had proposed less desirable names. I assume that my nickname, "Dusie" (rhymes with "Susie"), was some distorted derivative of my middle name and given to me to add to the discomfort of having an odd moniker culled from the last names of two notable African Americans, Dorothy Maynor and W.E.B. DuBois.

Going by my middle name and nickname was a two-for-one deal in complicating my social graces. Having to tell people my first name added no comfort in my attempts at telling people who I was. I did come to appreciate my name more when Momma told me that had I been born a girl, my name would have been Lucretia Cotillia.

In 1948, prior to our moving from 62 to 76 Polk Street, Obediah McCoy and his wife lived at our future home. Their tempestuous relationship ended violently soon after my brother Lafayette watched their silhouettes cast on a window shade. Moments later, the sound of a shotgun blast reverberated from the house through the neighborhood. Neighbors quickly investigated the incident. Mr. McCoy lay dead on the floor, bathed in a pool of blood. Among the curiosity-seekers was my sister, Billie, who escorted me, a three-year-old, to view the dead body. Eventually the ambulance and police arrived, clearing the crime scene.

Our living conditions at 62 Polk must have been dire indeed, because within a few days of the murder Momma had arranged for us to move into this very house. Considering that 76 had no electricity and represented a step up from our previous location, I can only imagine the condition of the house from which we moved. Since I was too young to recall witnessing the tragedy at what was to become our new home, I don't believe that the incident had any deleterious effect on my mental development.

My earliest recollections of living at 76 Polk, which stood at the corner of Polk and Garland streets, included playing with the Herndon boys, James, known by his middle name, Ben, and Silas, known by his middle name, Kent. Directly across the street from us in this tight-knit community lived the Patricks, who moved up the street shortly before we moved away. My five years of life were sandwiched between two of the Patrick children, Patricia, a year older, and Clarence ("Ba'y Bro"), a year younger. Two more Patrick children, Nancy and Joyce, were to follow.

Before the Patricks moved, their house had one feature missing from our five-room house: electric lights, punctuated by the dim incandescent porch-light bulb that served as my reminder of the haves and have-nots. A few houses in our block lacked electricity, yet I got little consolation out of this fact, because I saw the power of this utility and wanted it.

Polk Street, like most streets in our neighborhood, started at Hollins Street, the west side of which I believe has the longest continuous sidewalk in the city. Anyone living on Hollins Street was guaranteed to have a backyard that dropped dramatically toward the train tracks twenty to thirty feet below. The Lynch family lived on Hollins Street adjacent to the Fox family, who occupied the first house on our side of Polk Street. The original owner of the Fox house at 50 Polk Street was the elderly Nannie Wade, mother of Lucy Fox, the matriarch of the family. Miss Lucy, as she was called, worked at Lynchburg General Hospital, along with my mother and other neighborhood women.

Miss Lucy had two sons, Clifford and Paul, who were slightly older than I was. They were among the children who resided here. The Green family, whose son William, Jr., was to be one of my classmates, rented two rooms from the Foxes and had a private entrance to their residence. After the Greens moved to 1021 Hollins Street, Lula Tisdale and her two children, Donald and Ann, lived here.

The Fox house at 50 Polk Street

Next to the Fox family, at 52 Polk, lived the Hopkins family, which included children Milton, Garnet, and Annette. At 54 Polk Street lived the matronly Mrs. Hayes, who had relatives scattered throughout Tinbridge Hill. My close friend, James "Boodie" Anderson, lived next door at 56 Polk. Boodie lived with his father, Newman, and mother, Ida, one of my mother's friends. His older sister, Rosetta, also lived with them. His brother, Chris, would come along a few years later. The Andersons and our family worshipped at Fifth Street Baptist Church.

At 58 Polk Street lived the Campbells and their son, William "Billie Boy" Plummer, a double-jointed lad two or three years my junior, who later acquired the nickname "Goat" from the billy goats of fairy-tale fame. The Holmes family lived at 60 Polk Street, and the Rose family, kin to the

The women from Lynchburg General Hospital pose in this 1955 photo. Lucy Fox is sitting on the left.

Patricks, replaced us as the residents of 62 Polk Street. The final resident on this block on our side of the street was Ida Crawford, who lived at 64 Polk.

As Polk Street started its steep two-block descent to intersect with Second Street in the hollow, it passed the corner house of Wheeler and Ruby Hughes on Garland Street. Wheeler Hughes, Sr., was a legendary basketball star at Hampton Institute. My younger friend, Wheeler, Jr., known as "Wee Wee," was fed a diet of sports, at which he excelled. Next to the Hugheses on Garland Street was the Caul family, including children Leslie, Gracie, and the diminutive McKinley, whom we called "Boochie."

The Brimms lived next to them with children Ralph, who was about my brother Noon's age, and Wilton. I would become acquainted with two more Brimm brothers, Dennis and Roland, along with their sister, known as Sookie Jane, after we moved to McKinley Street.

Across from the Fox family lived George "Mr. Zeke" Hughes and his wife. Mr. Zeke was a member of the Hughes clan that has made so many significant contributions to Lynchburg's black community. I remember being about five years old and floating on an inner tube in ten feet of water at the Jefferson Park Pool, accompanied by Mr. Zeke, one of the most beloved neighbors in our community.

Next to Mr. Zeke lived two of my mother's friends, Vashti and Haywood Hopkins, and their children, Haywood, Jr., known as "Shug," and Yvonne ("Teeny"). Teeny was my age, and Haywood was closer to my sister's age. One of my fondest memories of being with them is a trip to a night baseball game at Lynchburg Stadium, the first time I had seen a professional event.

Since we had no automobile, I savored any outing involving getting into a vehicle. This excursion stands out because of the brilliance of the lights, which fascinated me even more than the athletic prowess of the baseball players.

The Patricks, who had recently moved from their bungalow at the corner of Polk and Garland, now lived almost at the peak of tree-lined Polk. They remained the owners of their former residence, converting its backyard lot into a small wood-selling business and later building the Midget Market, a neighborhood convenience store.

In the corner house, next to the Patricks, lived the elderly Mrs. Franklin, whom my mother would take me to visit. Mrs. Franklin lived in a gray two-story dwelling surrounded by high-growing privets. I felt as though I were going into a haunted house as Momma led me up the stairs where the bedridden Mrs. Franklin received consolation from my mother. My eyes tended to wander around the room, catching snippets of glass artifacts and collectibles from her past. We lived diagonally across the street from Mrs. Franklin, whose house exuded a forbidding aura, cautioning young, fragile imaginations to stay away. I believe my mother sensed my discomfort and began making solitary visits, leaving me to play alone in our yard.

The former Patrick house stayed unoccupied while we remained on Polk Street, leaving a gap in our block's population, which included the Dennis household, consisting of Mrs. Kate Dennis and her daughters Evelyn, who was about fifteen years older than I, and her older sister, Maggie. Mrs. Dennis had a movie projector on which she would show silent films of slapstick comedy.

Mr. Wilson's store, a small bungalow tightly squeezed between the Dennis house and another bungalow, had limited space for shoppers. Between the front door and the glass counter, Wilson's Store could comfortably accommodate no more than three adults or five small children. I paid scant attention to the dry goods sold beyond the candy counter. As long as I could have my diet of Mary Janes, BB Bats, Mint Juleps, Johnny Cakes, licorice, and other sweets, nothing else mattered.

As Polk Street sloped down to Second Street, so do my memories of Polk Street residents. I knew other people lived down the street, but I never had a lot of exposure to them.

The sun did not consistently shine during these halcyon days of early childhood. I attended Mary Bethune Nursery school at 1500 Floyd Street.

In 1936 the New Deal Works Progress Administration had opened Bethune Nursery School to give work and to allow inexpensive day care for African American families.

Bethune Nursery School provided both a foundation for my education and post-toddler trauma. As I played alone with wooden building blocks, one of my playmates, Joe, for who knows what reason, blurted out, "Aww... You said a bad word." Mildly shocked after realizing that no one else was close to him, I denied the accusation, asking him, "What did I say?"

Joe responded, "I can't say it, but you said a bad word." By this time, our playmate Betty Jean had come within earshot and, with no evidence whatsoever, echoed what Joe had said to our caregiver, who confronted me. I denied saying anything, while Joe again stated that I had said the phantom word.

The caregiver gently chastised me for using bad language, and I went back to playing with building blocks. Frustrated by my inability to prove my innocence, I was determined not to open my mouth. It didn't matter. Once again, Joe, as though pre-recorded, iterated the same claim against my character. To make matters worse, Betty Jean once more heard Joe and spread the tale to the caregiver.

For a few minutes I questioned my sanity. Had I really said a bad word without realizing it? In an instant, I came to my senses, realizing that I hadn't said anything and maybe someone else was a little off.

When I got home, I told Momma that Joe had "told a story" on me. I didn't say "lie" because, for me, that word in itself was a "bad" word. She believed me, and after her talk with the nursery school attendants, I never had another incident with Joe.

One other nursery school incident fills the dark side of my memory. This one was physically painful. Two boys attacked me while I slept on my bunk bed. Using the metal braces that supported our beds, they pounded my arms and back, while I sniveled under the protection of my wool blanket. I told Momma about the incident, and, though she expressed sympathy, she chided me for not defending myself.

These incidents failed to distract me from the joy of going to nursery school. Playing with toys, blocks, and other children overshadowed these examples of childhood callousness.

This Old House

In 1950, only a few months before my sixth birthday, I found out we were moving to McKinley Street. The first question I asked Momma was, "Will we have lights?" She assured me that electricity would now be part of our lifestyle. No longer would I have to clean soot from fragile glass lampshades that cracked under the assault of my still-developing fine motor skills. No more would my tender fingers douse the flames of an errantly adjusted lamp wick. And no longer would I have to be concerned about getting another eleven stitches under my eye from falling on an oilcan.

The prospect of having electricity came with a tradeoff. Acquiring this utility meant we would be sacrificing another: indoor plumbing. We had given up a sink and tub for a back-porch toilet and a spigot in the yard near the back porch steps. The "back" porch was a misnomer, for the porch extended from the side door of the kitchen.

Our toilet was one grade up from the outhouse located at Momma's family home in Big Island, Virginia. To supplement our bathroom facilities, we kept a porcelain chamber pot, which had to be replaced frequently because of my careless handling. The chamber pot was handy when the temperature dropped; sitting on an ice-cold back-porch toilet seat required a small act of courage.

If temperatures were cold enough, the water in our commode froze. Sometimes I forgot about this phenomenon until I flushed my business, which would go everywhere except down the drain. Sometimes, as a caution, we cut off the water supply to the commode tank, preventing such mishaps, or we heated water to pour into the frozen toilet.

When I first saw our new digs, I was oblivious to the downgrade in our dwelling. As far as I was concerned, having electricity trumped any domiciliary tradeoff. The fact that we now had a four-room house instead of a five-room house didn't bother me. Having outdoor plumbing and living in the worst house on the street were tolerable. By contrast, my sister, in shock, queried when she saw the drab gray structure, "We're going to live in that shack?" I didn't care, because we had ELECTRICITY!

Our house was built on the sloping landscape of McKinley Street. The west end of our small front porch was at ground level, while the east end stopped about three feet above the yard. The height of the back porch, which extended from the west side of the kitchen, increased proportionately and created a crawl space where our heating and cooking fuels were stored.

We had two doors to our crawl space. The one under the front room opened to the space allotted for kindling—scrap wood we bought by the tub. The lower, taller door opened to the space reserved for coal, deposited by way of a conveyor belt on the delivery truck, and for oil, which was stored in three fifty-five-gallon drums. Later, the oil drums would be removed and placed outside on stands below the kitchen window.

Though the crawl space was all dirt, I found it a source of exploratory fantasies. I would venture from the back end, first standing, then stooping, as I made my way under the front porch. Then I crawled, either on my back or face down, turning my head to the side to achieve maximum distance. I was never able to reach my final destination, the far end of the porch, because the angle became too narrow.

Sometimes I would dream that the space was deeper and I had succeeded in traversing the whole area. Then I would wake up, believing it was possible, and crawl under the porch again to see if my dream could become a reality. It never did.

I had other dreams that dealt with home improvement as I adjusted to our have-nots. In one recurring dream we had indoor plumbing and a door that led directly from the commode to the kitchen. Each time I awoke, I would be disappointed, knowing that a washbasin and a number-three wash tub in the kitchen were the closest I would get to my dream.

My brothers, who were eight and six years older than I, slept in a regular-size bed in our bedroom above the front room. I slept on an army cot, complete with a rubber blanket to hold my bed-wetting urine. My bladder had some sort of circadian rhythm, allowing me to stay dry during summer nights and opening my sphincters during the coldest of winter days.

Because of the poor insulation, we had a small wood stove attached to the chimney that ran up the middle of the house. For our comfort and convenience, we shared a porcelain chamber pot with Momma and Billie, who slept in the other bedroom.

Momma's bedroom provided an intriguing view of parts of Rivermont Avenue, about a twenty-five-minute walk from our house. When the sun set, the light would reflect off a many-paned building, giving the impression that it was on fire. This phenomenon often mesmerized me, because each time I saw it, knowing it was an illusion, something inside of me kept believing that I should be hearing fire alarms. It was only when the sun set further that I would come to my senses. Out of habit, though, when the phenomenon happened again, my mind went through the same sequence of impressions.

Technology Makeover

Anticipation of turning on lights gave me giddy feelings. Despite the protestations of my sister, I felt that my class status had increased. After adjusting to pulling the light-switch cord to our barren ceiling bulb, I discovered other benefits of this fantastic utility.

To make space for potential electrical appliances and gadgets, remnants of a past life had to fade into oblivion. We had brought our wood-burning kitchen stove, on which we heated non-electric irons that could scorch shirts and blister hands in an instant. Our icebox and foot-pedaled Singer sewing machine survived on borrowed time, while new appliances lounged in Schewel's Furniture Store, waiting for their chance to add comfort and convenience to our lives.

Besides basic light bulbs, I don't know what domestic changes were priorities. I'd like to think my relationship to the movies played a starring role in the decision to get an electric range.

I was eight years old when I found a live .38-caliber bullet and wanted to remove the gunpowder so that I could use it to replay a recurring scene in B-westerns. My goal was to make a short trail of gunpowder that I could light in the manner of cowboys blowing up kegs of dynamite.

Without regard for likely dismemberment, I tried to pry the shell casing from the bullet with a screwdriver and pliers. Failing to do this, I thought that if beat the shell with a hammer, I would have more success. My brother Cutchie had told me that as long as I didn't hit the base of the shell, I'd be safe. Confident in this knowledge, I pounded and pulled that shell, which refused to cooperate. The casing held fast to the bullet, denying me my opportunity at pyrotechnics.

Frustrated and still wanting satisfaction, I placed the live bullet in the blazing kitchen stove, quietly slipped back into the yard, and waited. In a few minutes, I heard the sound of a gunshot, followed by the clanging of one of the iron lids on the stovetop. Momma was in the kitchen when this event occurred and vehemently scolded me. I neither confirmed nor denied my involvement, but I knew, since I didn't get a whipping for my prank, that I had dodged the real bullet. Shortly afterward, a new General Electric range replaced the old stove, a GE electric iron reduced the old irons to doorstops, and a GE refrigerator occupied the ice-box corner.

Now that we had electric outlets, Momma made sure that we had something to plug into them. She bought a Philco Hi-Fidelity record player that allowed me to discriminate between treble and bass. My preference was to listen to those fragile 78-rpm records that everybody in my house bought except for me.

A radio had preceded the record player, giving me my first exposure to easy-listening WLVA but denying me the pleasure of "race" music—rhythm 'n' blues—until about 1954, when we got our first black disc jockey, Starling Merritt, on WBRG.

To cool us in the summer, Momma bought a small oscillating fan with four-inch blades. This fan became part of my

In 1954, Aunt Julia bought me this copy of "My Blue Heaven" by Fats Domino. It was the first record I ever owned.

many unsanctioned scientific experiments, allowing me to satisfy my curiosity about aerodynamics. I tested a variety of materials—paper, string, bobby pins—for their ability to enter the back vortex of the fan and be expelled from the front. I never had a scientific breakthrough, though I did have fun watching my hodgepodge of baubles hit the fan.

My brother Lafayette, as a teenaged sailor, stands in our yard in front of the DeLoatch home. The wisteria vines behind him hide the privets that were used as punishment for my mischief.

For our bedroom, Momma bought table lamps, another source of botched experiments. I discovered how to shock myself by screwing in light bulbs while the lamp was still on. I tested the effect of dropping hair and bobby pins into live lamp sockets and observed what happened when I placed a penny in the lamp socket and watched sparks fly after turning on the power. To satisfy my curiosity about the conductibility of copper, I placed a penny in the lamp socket and screwed in a light bulb. Instead of witnessing blinding luminescence, I saw the lamp socket turn metallic black and blue and the filament in the bulb burn to a crisp. Playing with electricity was like being in Edison's Menlo Park. And I lived to tell about it.

A string-pulled light switch controlled each ceiling light. If one of the switches went bad, Momma called Clifford Fox to make the repair. Clifford was a teenage tinker who had a reputation for making minor repairs and creating useful gadgets. I had no knowledge of how to fix anything, though I was an expert in disassembling almost everything. Clifford was an example of how we pooled community resources and helped each other.

Momma bought a Warm Morning stove for the front room, and contrary to what I believed was the intent of this baby coal furnace—to heat up the room—it served a more selfish purpose and heated only itself. As long as we huddled around the stove, we stayed comfortable. Move one foot away, or sit down, and the temperature dropped forty-eight degrees.

By the winter of 1955, when Noon had enrolled in Hampton Institute and Cutchie had enlisted in the Navy, I assumed the task of tending to the needs of this coal-eater. If I failed to take care of this spoiled stove, it would punish me by refusing to ignite the coal after I fed it kindling. My frustration with this inanimate object reached a climax when I, an impatient twelve-year-old, prepped the stove with paper and kindling with the expectation of an output of increased British Thermal Units. Instead, the flames failed to materialize—not even a smolder.

Cautiously, I resulted to my backup plan: kerosene. Knowing the volatility of this liquid, I poured a little on my pyre, made sure the vents were open, then tossed in a lighted match while swiftly closing the top loading door. I expected a minor explosion that would be buffered by the lining of the stove, but, to be on the safe side, I jumped back after tossing the match. Nothing happened. I waited a few seconds before curiosity got the best of me.

I opened the door and peeked inside. Before I could catch my breath, the delayed whoosh I had expected roared out of the stove. My head instantly snapped back as visions of a toasted face entered my life history. My reaction time was fast enough for me to avoid any burns, though something in the room had changed. I could smell burnt hair and, without any further thought, knew that the stove had exacted punishment by singeing my hair. I chuckled to myself as I felt my brittle widow's peak crumble down my face. Thinking that this was the extent of my toasting, I rubbed my hand across my eyes and watched my eyelashes fall the way of my hair. From then on, I had more respect for the power of fossil fuel, whatever its form.

Momma bought a Siegler oil stove for the kitchen to compensate for the lack of heat produced by the electric range. The kitchen heated up better than the front room, probably because in the kitchen we had only one set of windows from which cold air seeped in, as opposed to the two windows in the front room and the cracks around the seams of the front door. The problem was that the kitchen was less inviting as a family meeting place. I would have preferred placing the oil stove in the front room and turning the heat and blower as high as possible than pretending to be warmed by that narcissistic brown monster that posed as a stove.

Washing clothes took on new meaning with the addition of a wringer washing machine that Momma placed on the back porch. Each cycle of the wash produced a signature sound. I would stare hypnotically as the churned clothes beat out a drum-like rhythm worthy of musical improvisation. The rinse cycle hissed out a stream of fresh water, while the drain cycle depended on the precise placement of the drain hose, or water would gurgle randomly all over the porch.

The rollers of the wringer caused me to wonder how much pain I would suffer if I stuck my hand between them. As tempting as this was, seeing clothes flatten out when guided through the wringer convinced me to keep my hands to myself. Ronnie Douglas had the distinction of being the first person in our neighborhood to test the power of the wringer. His bandaged hand provided the final proof that washing machines should be respected.

By the mid 1950s, Lynchburg was making a push to get houses up to plumbing codes. I watched as Mr. McDaniel expanded the bathroom area off his kitchen to include a bathtub and other improvements. Miss Elaine made similar improvements, as did the Scott family. Pappy DeLoatch had already installed code-approved plumbing. Our house remained the only dwelling on our street without decent plumbing.

It was inevitable that our plumbing would fall in line with the rest of the neighborhood, or so I thought, but Momma had other ideas. Our landlord could upgrade our plumbing; however, that would mean increasing the rent. Considering our economic status, increased rent was not an option, so the opportunity to have a house with indoor plumbing eluded us for the duration of our decade on McKinley Street.

As I got older, I became more sensitive to living in the only house on our street without indoor plumbing. Several times I dreamed that our kitchen had been remodeled, having a sink, in which I washed dishes, and a door from the kitchen leading to a real bathroom that contained a tub with hot and cold water. My dreams seemed so real that I did not want to wake up to the reality of turning on a faucet handle attached a two-inch-diameter pipe that rose about three feet from the surface of our yard.

Our communication with the outside world broadened when, in 1954, we got a telephone. Most families in our community had phones. The earlier phone owners had party lines, which were cheaper, but our household opted for a private line and the latest model.

I anticipated making my first phone call when, in the fourth grade, my mind was more occupied with talking to my friends than with paying attention to my lessons. When I got home from school in gleeful anticipation, everyone else in the family had made his or her inaugural call. Now it was my turn.

My family gathered around the end table where the phone stood. I was poised for that memorable moment. I dialed Junie and then lifted the receiver, waiting to make history like Alexander Graham Bell to Thomas Watson. I waited for the phone to ring, only to hear the dial tone. Helplessly I held the receiver while my sister, Billie, pointed out my procedural error: "You have to pick up the receiver before you dial."

I had blown my opportunity to get it right the first time. This letdown made dialing Junie anti-climactic. The simple act of dialing a telephone—I had failed, and there would be no second chance for a first impression. How Charlie Brown could I be?

Television would have to wait until 1956. Until then, I had to listen to the radio or rely on the kindness of the McDaniels and Miss Elaine, who would let me watch television with their families. Once we got that twenty-one-inch Zenith, I was immediately hooked, scheduling chores and homework around my favorite shows. It would be years before I could wean myself from the seduction of this plugged-in drug.

Owning a television completed our technology upgrade. On the downside, the television added to my isolation, because I had one less reason to visit my friends at night. On the upside, it gave me something else to talk about and increased my awareness of culture beyond Lynchburg.

A Fuel's Errand

Our house used diverse sources of fuel to meet our cooking and heating needs. The chimney that ran up the middle of the house had three stoves with stovepipes that fed into it. This was a change from our house on Polk Street, where we relied on a smokestack jutting from the back of the house to indiscriminately release smoke and ashes into the environment.

Our kitchen, warmed by the dependable Siegler, got heating oil from two sources. The main source was the three fifty-five-gallon oil drums located in the crawl space under the kitchen. If these drums ran dry, then I had to go to either Hayslett's or Cochran's store and buy two gallons of oil.

We had glass gallon jugs that I transported from the stores to home, a mere five blocks away. At age eight or nine, I had neither the strength nor the endurance in my puny fingers to carry the oil more than a half a block without aches and pains. By the time I got to the white Carl Miller's house at Federal and Garland streets, my fingers so ached from the pressure that I would set the jugs under one of the maple trees that lined the sidewalk in front of his yard.

I would take time to gather myself, because after I rounded the curb, stopping at the Simpsons' house before heading towards Phillips' Store (formerly known as Phillips' Coffee Shop), I knew that there would be no more soft areas on which to rest the delicate glass jugs.

If I had no caps for the bottles, by the time I got home my pants would reek of the oil that had sloshed out during my trek. Even worse, if I accidentally allowed the bottles to collide during a finger exchange, or set one down too abruptly, then I would wind up delivering one bottle to

Momma instead of two. Eventually we got metal cans with more ergonomic grips, making my journey safer and more pleasant.

Having oil drums under our house kept our fuel dry but posed a fire hazard. Most of the time, getting oil from our drum was not a big deal. Problems arose when I forgot to monitor the oil levels of the stove and had to fill the glass jugs at night.

Each of the three spigots had its unique characteristic. Two were operated with turn-screws that allowed me to regulate the flow of oil into the jugs. The mouth of the jug fit conveniently over the mouth of the spigot; I would turn the spigot wide open and watch the oil foam as it gushed into the bottle. I had to time the flow in order to keep the oil from overflowing, which it often did. The two spigots did not flow at the same rate, making it more difficult to gauge my timing.

The third spigot had a lever that I pressed to allow the oil to flow. I preferred this lever to the turn-screws because once I took my hand off it, the oil stopped flowing. The only drawback to this system was that the mouth of the spigot did not fit neatly into the jug, so if I were not careful, oil would spray all over the ground and me.

These oil drums revealed both a dark and an enlightened side to my character. One night when I was ten, our oil supply had almost run out. If we were going to have heat, I would have to squeeze the final bit from the lever-action drum.

The drums rested on wooden frames that allowed me to tilt the barrels in order to get the final drops from the container. The flashlight that I usually took with me under the house had weak batteries, so I had to feel my way in the dark.

In order to complete my task, I had to tilt the barrel while pressing the lever and holding the jug under the spout. It was difficult to accomplish all these maneuvers at once. When I tilted the barrel while leaning it against my shoulder, I could put the jug under the spigot, but I could not press the lever that released the oil. When I tried to press the lever, my shoulder moved, causing the barrel to tilt backwards and me to release my grip. Or, worse, I pressed the lever and the jug slipped from the spigot just as the oil started to flow, spilling on the ground and me.

After a series of permutations and combinations in incompetence, I did something consciously and deliberately for the first time in my life: out of anger and frustration, I uttered my first curse word: "Shit!"

Suddenly, neural pathways not connected to the restricted area of my auditory memory opened a Pandora's box of profanity. Words I had hitherto repressed flowed from my lips as if I had discovered the Rosetta stone of bad words. I began to say aloud words that all my friends used with ease, and I said them without any measure of guilt.

After sating my brain with expletives, I felt ready to share my cursing acumen with my friends. But how could I make this transition, considering that no one had ever heard me say words that had never before been part of my vocabulary?

The next day I was around Paul, who had a reputation for blending cuss words into almost every sentence that came out of his mouth, and Bill, who used profanity sparingly. During the course of our normal conversation, I uttered my first public four-letter expletive. Paul looked at me nonplussed and said, "Oh, so when did you start cussing?"

At that moment, I realized that my entrance into the world of profanity placed me in a state of cognitive dissonance. Though I was comfortable saying the words in the privacy of the crawl space, they conflicted with my natural reticence. Recognizing that my character had slid downhill, I reverted to my old ways and would not consciously utter profanity for another eighteen years.

Linking spirituality to drawing oil in the dark is like going through six degrees of separation. One day as I waited for my oil jug to fill, I began forming thoughts in my head about speaking a foreign language. In a few moments, I uttered syllables in crystal clarity that seemed to make sense to me, although I could not interpret them. In amazement, I uttered a few more syllables, and soon the words started flowing like the oil in my jug.

Fascinated by this phenomenon, I let my tongue take over my mind as I reached a heightened state of awareness I had never attained before. For about fifteen minutes I allowed myself to speak these utterances whose meanings seemed to be on the tip of my tongue. Alone under the house, I realized that other people were missing out on my amazing ability and wished someone were available to witness it. Soon these utterances merged with the reality of supplying our oil stove with the necessary fuel. Though I wanted to continue this foreign conversation with myself, I reluctantly terminated my talk, which I never attempted again. This marked my first and last experience with glossolalia, commonly referred to as speaking in tongues.

I attribute this phenomenon to no specific religious alignment. Rather, glossolalia represented an untapped area of my brain and an ability, if I put my mind to it, that I could use to raise my level of consciousness. However, in no other time in my life did I make an effort to speak in tongues, though a few religious leaders with Pentecostal backgrounds have tried to encourage me to do so.

When we ran out of kindling, fuel for starting fires in the Warm Morning came from an alternate source. Sometimes I scoured the neighboring woods for kindling, bundling it in the manner of Native Americans. If we ran out of wood in the summer, I would pull a piece of rotted plank from the crawl space of our house and burn it as a kindling substitute.

Pulling rotten wood from the side of our house served a two-fold purpose: it gave us ready-to-use firewood, and it forced replacement of the planks of rotten wood near our crawl space. Momma hardly objected because along with our kindling we were always getting planks that made suitable replacements.

Times like these showed the disparity in resources between our neighbors and us. Whenever I had to face the world lacking what others took for granted, I always found comfort in knowing that I had a certain peace within myself. I knew the world was larger and offered more than I had on McKinley Street, yet when I was alone, my world was limited only by my imagination. As long as I kept a foothold on my sanity, I could endure the pitfalls of shyness and economic poverty.

The Terrain of My Domain

T he geography and terrain of our community added to the distinct features of McKinley Street. I don't know the complete history of the street, but I consider it one of the most unusual streets anywhere.

To convey its uniqueness, I will describe the street's physical features, adding houses on the neighboring streets—Hollins, Federal, and McIvor—to allow readers to visualize this much neglected and underappreciated area of Lynchburg. The map on page iv represents my memory of the place.

View of Blackwater Creek from Hollins Mill Road, near the railroad tunnel

Hollins Mill dam

As Blackwater Creek meanders toward the James River, it carves a thumb-like projection with ridges that overlook the creek nearly one hundred fifty feet below. The Hollins Mill Road bridge, which spans Blackwater Creek, serves as a natural dividing line between the Rivermont section of town and Tinbridge Hill. From the bridge—the tip of the thumb—to the beginning of McKinley Street—the base— the elevation rises close to two hundred feet. The natural terrain of this area was a major factor in shaping the quality of my life.

The construction of McKinley Street seemed to be a result of poor planning or was perhaps another way to show contempt for those who would live there. Apparently, the street was to have formed a semicircle around the second block of Federal Street, beginning at the northeast corner of Lynchburg General Hospital and exiting at the next corner.

An early map of the area (See page ii) reveals a continuous street making an irregular loop behind the second block of Federal Street. The northern entrance is labeled McKinley (North Bend), and the part of McKinley Street we lived on is referred to as Norvell Street.

By the time our family arrived in 1950, the loop had been broken for years, and few vestiges of a continuous street remained. The terrain yielded no evidence that any construction had ever taken place to join the two ends of the street. Instead, McKinley Street began as an unmarked driveway where Hollins Street merged with Federal Street, which at that point became Hollins Mill Road. Part of this nondescript driveway branched upward into the yard of the Douglas family, which occupied the house on Federal Street across the street from the southeast corner of the hospital. The main entrance to this part of McKinley Street veered right, descending past and separating the Douglas house from the Morris house, which represented the transition of Federal Street from a white to a black neighborhood.

Street maintenance for McKinley ended at the sidewalk ramp bordering the beginning of the street. Only ruts shaped by the few vehicles that ventured down this sparsely graveled dead-end driveway defined McKinley as a street. None of the houses on this part of McKinley had either indoor plumbing or electricity, lowering their status one grade below our house.

While the left side of the entrance rose along the Douglas yard, which children occasionally used as a shortcut to the other side of McKinley Street, the ersatz street itself descended along a ridge containing four primitive houses on its right side. To the left of the street was a brushy hill overgrown with saplings of the utilitarian tree of heaven, commonly known as the stinkwood tree for its awful smell.

The Austins occupied the first dwelling on McKinley Street. Randolph ("Rand"), who was my age, and his younger sister, Lillian ("Lee"), lived with their mother and the local black golf legend we called "Skin Tom." Their rustic cedar house seemed more suitable for a farm than for urban life. They had fewer conveniences of urban life than we did. Their yard sloped down to a ravine where, on the other side, a makeshift dump marked the beginning of the dead-end of Harrison Street.

A crude sidewalk made of stone slabs separated the undeveloped road from the remaining three houses. Each of these houses became more precarious as the slope on which it was built grew steeper. Their back ends were supported by weathered four-by-four-inch stilts, which left little room for construction error. Each time I walked past these houses, I marveled at their ability to defy gravity, knowing that should any one of the supports give way, an entire house would crumble.

Urban legend Willie Lightning, whose extremely everted lower lip cause him to drool constantly, lived in the house next to the Austins. We heard he had burned his lip on a stove, which sounded more colorful than having a birth defect.

Willie did a lot of yard work throughout the city and would often be seen wielding a sickle, which he carried most of the time, around the edges of some prominent white families' homes on Garland Hill. Momma sometimes allowed him to cut around our yard, giving him sandwiches to tide him over.

Children believed that if you agitated Willie Lightning, he would lop off your head with his sickle. With childlike insensitivity, we cautiously taunted him from a safe distance, mentally mapping out our escape routes in case he decided to chase us. He rarely took more that a few steps in our direction before we scattered like the wind.

We also tormented Willie with another childish activity. Out of boredom or impishness, we would hide near a the grove of trees lining the southwest side of Willie's house and lob rocks or clods of dirt onto his roof. We would throw our missiles high in the air and run from the scene before they pounded his house. As we approached our teen years, we ceased this activity.

On the hill opposite Willie Lightning's house grew native flora, including the pungent stinkwood trees, briars, composites, milkweed, and goldenrod. Depending on crop rotation, the field that arose from the slope of this terrain became corn or whatever crop Mr. Douglas saw fit to plant. The elevation of this area peaked and then plateaued, forming a natural boundary to the lot we generically referred to as "the Field."

At the end of Willie Lightning's house, McKinley Street began its devolution from a navigable roadway to a series of pathways that branched to all parts of the ridge on which we lived. Following the most logical

View of Blackwater Creek from a slope below McIvor Street

pathway to where the street might have been would lead to circling behind the house of the McDaniel family to a clearing that sloped upward and connected to the dead end of the most recognized portion of McKinley Street.

Once this path began to look like a street, the roadway slowly elevated, reaching its peak at the Johnson house, and then descended abruptly, connecting back to Federal Street, without a street sign indicating location or warning of no thoroughfare. The last block of houses on Federal Street drifted to the right as the street assumed the identity of Hollins Mill Road.

Before Hollins Mill Road made its grand descent toward Blackwater Creek, it yielded another side street, McIvor, which crested along the ridge before plummeting behind the Isbell estate in its cul-de-sac. As Hollins Mill Road gradually twisted downward, McIvor Street held its course about thirty feet higher than its more famous progenitor. The right side of McIvor Street grew steeper toward the cul-de-sac; there, vine-entangled trees growing along the slope competed for precious sunlight.

The ridge at the peak of McIvor Street dropped at least one hundred eighty feet to the banks of Blackwater Creek, forming a natural playground for boys who liked to explore reticulated pathways, climb jagged rocks, or swing on wrist-thick vines attached to massive hardwood trees.

Essentially, then, our community consisted of three streets, the two dysfunctional dead ends of McKinley Street and the cul-de-sac McIvor, each of which owed some allegiance to Federal Street, which changed its name as it began a final winding trek toward Blackwater Creek. By default, the first block of Harrison Street was also considered part of our community, since it shared demographic characteristics with our dead-end streets.

On the east side of Federal Street a retaining wall had been built along the sidewalk beginning at the Douglas house and increasing in height past the next two houses as the street elevation declined. "The Wall," as we called it, made a short drop, draped by bushes, and stopped at the end of the block at the site we called "the Foundation," which was the remnant of a corner lot home at 36 McKinley Street. Miss Elaine told me that an impressive house had once stood on this site but had fallen into disrepair when the owner moved out and then salvaged wood from the house to repair another house that had been damaged in a fire. The Foundation became a gathering place for children and a source of raw material for homemade bows and arrows.

Next to the Douglas house was the home of Mr. Jesse Ward, seldom seen unless we happened to be sitting on his part of the Wall, which we often did. Mr. Jesse, as he was called, had a concrete driveway that made a car-wide rift in the Wall. When we walked the Wall, we often jumped from the Douglas side hoping to land on Mr. Jesse's side, but the gap was too wide.

Mr. Jesse's part of the Wall served as a meeting place whenever we heard ambulance sirens headed toward the hospital. The Wall faced the emergency room, and if our timing was right, we could get a glimpse of the latest trauma to arrive. Our darkest wish was to see as much blood as possible so we could describe the gory details to anyone who might have missed the excitement.

Two things some of us did in front of Mr. Jesse's house were criminal. The emergency room housed vending machines holding snacks and drinks for hospital workers. Since we could enter this area unimpeded, we often made use of the machines. When we ran out of money, we would search under the machines, looking for errant coins. If our searches proved fruitless, then we sometimes took pennies and, using Mr. Jesse's wall, filed them to the size and shape of dimes. We would then use the counterfeit coins to purchase our favorite packs of Nabs.

Since the driveway to the emergency room allowed no public parking, soft-drink trucks parked on the side of Federal Street where we made our dimes. The drinks were uncovered and tempted us to no end. Whenever one of us discovered that a drink truck had arrived, he, like a dutiful scout, would spread the word. We would wait for the driver to leave his truck unattended; then, like ants swarming to a lump of sugar, we would descend on the truck and make off with RC Colas or Nehi soft drinks. Seldom did any of us urchins take more than one. Eventually, the driver got wise and stayed in the truck while a helper, usually a black man, restocked the drink machines.

The hospital offered its own set of perks for our neighborhood. Besides providing steady employment for many people on Tinbridge Hill, it also supplemented our food source. On Friday nights, Momma would take us through the emergency room, where we gained access to the kitchen and pilfered any leftovers from the prior week's meals. The children would head for the ice cream freezer, selecting ice cream sandwiches and Neapolitan ice cream blocks, delicacies for my eight-year-old palate. In the meantime, Momma collected meats and other staples, which she shared with Miss Elaine and others who might be in need. Sometimes while making our rounds we would meet Clifford and Paul Fox and other children accompanying parents who were employed here. Once the hospital relocated to Tate Springs Road in the mid-1950s, we were unable to continue this practice.

Next to Mr. Jesse's house stood the most transitional dwelling in our neighborhood, a double tenement house I remember mostly for its dark hallways and the host of children who came in and out of my life. They included my early classmates Betty Jean Ferguson and Gloria Jean and Fred Smith; the Davis family, with Florence, the mother, and children Helen, Bobby, Jack, and Carl; Edith Crews with children Reginald ("Roughhouse") and Ricky; the Hubbards, with children Mary, Linda, and Mark; the Gentry family, with daughters Maxine and Joyce; and the Halls, with mother Castle, son Junie, and daughters Mildred Ann and Glenda. Also making frequent visits was the flamboyant Woodrow Hall, who was known for his repartee and colorful aphorisms, such as "Speed on before you get peed on."

The entranceway to the Foundation included two flights of concrete steps to nowhere, used as a gathering place. Sometimes we scared unsuspecting pedestrians by jumping out from behind the steps that were embedded in the hillside. On the first flight of steps, we often played "one potato, two potato," while on the landing between the two flights the more social children played "post office" and "spin the bottle," games I considered yucky at my immature age.

The second flight of steps, our little Mt. Everest, offered a crow's nest view, though a limited one, of the neighborhood. In the wintertime, I could look south through the bare trees and get a glimpse of the high trestle that spanned the huge gap between Tinbridge Hill and Rivermont. Looking down into the Foundation, I could picture the outline of the missing house that now resembled a bombed-out building from World War II. If I turned my sights closer to home, I could see the rest of the houses on McKinley Street.

The wall around the Foundation was suitable for testing our balance and nerve. The low side (as we called it) of the wall was at ground level, but the high side—the McKinley Street side—rose high enough to challenge risk-takers. The gutted windows formed gaps we could cross only by jumping down and then climbing up again. Rather than walk across the gap, we usually opted to jump inside the Foundation or into the surrounding brush-covered pathway. The inside of the Foundation was littered with household debris, making exploration a dangerous scavenger hunt.

As McKinley Street began its ascent from Federal Street to residential life, the Johnsons lived in the first house on the right side of the street. Miss Elaine lived with her elderly mother, Mrs. Laura Smith, who owned the house. Previously, Miss Elaine had lived at 24 Federal Street, the house where she got married. Miss Elaine had smooth skin, short hair, and high cheekbones that hinted of a Native American ancestry.

Her tight four-room one-story bungalow on McKinley Street always had both children and adults flowing in and out. My playmates included Mary ("Bumpsie"), her younger sister Brenda ("Boo Boo"), and Reginald ("Bud"), whom we mistakenly called "Bugs", and Lillian Smith, Miss Elaine's niece.

One of the most colorful people to live with Miss Elaine was her brother, Calvin, who had the silkiest voice I had ever heard. Anyone who ever heard him sing swore he was Nat "King" Cole. We would encourage him to sign a stanza of "Mona Lisa" or "Darling, Je Vous Aime Beacoup," imagining that he was sitting behind a baby grand piano or in front of an NBC microphone. "Why don't you sing professionally?" we would ask him. His pat answer was always "I'm too shy to get on stage and sing in front of a lot of people." I wished that some impresario would tap his talent so I could say that I knew a real star.

Miss Elaine, the matriarch of the family, had a chicken coop in her unfenced back yard and raised feisty Bantam chickens, including a rooster with a Napoleonic complex. This rooster strutted around his domain, chasing human interlopers without fear of reprisal. The Johnson yard became one of many shortcuts I used to get off McKinley Street, which we called "the Hill."

A short dirt driveway separated Miss Elaine's house from the Foundation. Sometimes her visitors would leave their cars unattended there. For Bumpsie's visiting father, this practice set the stage for a minor disaster. One day Bumpsie, who was about seven, decided that she was going to drive his car, with total disregard for the direction it faced—which was toward the Foundation. Miraculously, though she drove off the hill over into the Foundation, she escaped the crash with no injuries. The car, on the other hand, had to be hauled out of the Foundation while the neighborhood looked on.

After passing the Johnson house, McKinley Street started its descent to the unannounced dead end. The hub of the street, the lot known as the Field, separated the Johnsons' house at 15 McKinley from the imitation-brick-shingled McDaniel home at 9 McKinley, the only other house on that side of the street.

The Field took on different personalities depending on the season and the need for corn. Starting as a small embankment on McKinley Street, the Field rose in elevation, providing a panorama of the city. As the elevation peaked before it sloped down to the clearing sometimes used by Mr. Douglas for planting corn, it gave us a clear view of the Peaks of Otter in Bedford County, about thirty miles away. My young next-door neighbor, Bonnie, once pointed out how that part of the Blue Ridge Mountains looked liked a naked lady lying on her back.

The Field also gave us a clear view of the Jones Memorial Library, which I was convinced was a clone of Monticello as seen on the back of the nickel. I wanted to explore this library, but in the 1950s segregation kept me out.

On the other side of the street, four yards dropped like terraces, adjusting to the sloping lots on which the houses were built. Shortly after we arrived, the city replaced the stone slabs on our side of the street with a concrete sidewalk that went only as far as the first two houses. I guess the city ran out of concrete when it got to our house. Our "sidewalk" dropped suddenly as the concrete sidewalk ended and spacing between the remaining slabs dictated the need for a more demanding level of pedestrian finesse.

My most awkward interaction with the sidewalk occurred when I had to escort a blind caner to our house to put new seats in our wooden kitchen chairs. He had told me to let him know when to step up or down, or when the sidewalk was uneven. At age seven I was still possessed by shyness that compromised my ability to speak to adults. When it came time for me to indicate that the caner needed to step down from the sidewalk, my lips remained sealed. I had hoped that somehow he would know what to do. He didn't. Only by gripping my shoulder more tightly did he avoid disaster as his foot failed to hit solid ground. He scolded me for my lack of sensitivity, and I scolded myself for being so timid.

Pedestrians continued to negotiate our rudimentary sidewalk until the city paved our gravel street with asphalt and replaced the stone slabs with some of the excess material.

In the first house on this side of the street, across from Miss Elaine, lived the crusty Ms. Phoebe McIvor, whose small white one-story bungalow was filled with a glass menagerie. Her three-foot-high wire fence formed a sanctuary for stray balls, which she occasionally refused to return. As the street sloped, hedges lined the natural break in the terrain between her yard and that of her next-door neighbors, the Warrens.

Our house cascaded from the makeshift fence Mr. Warren made of spare tin boards and other scrap material used to keep his ground from eroding or washing into our yard after hard rains. Our compact front yard continued the declining slope and was hostile to grass, favoring dirt more suitable for my marble-shooting skills.

The complex Simon-DeLoatch family lived next door. Led by the venerable "Pappy" DeLoatch, a jack-of-all-trades handyman, the DeLoatch family included a diverse combination of relatives whose connections I could never accurately figure out. Pappy, whose physical shortcomings included a missing thumb and a pronounced limp, often logged home scrap lumber for home improvement projects.

A tale of Pappy's disabilities involved a case of mistaken identity. In his younger days the police were referred to as roaches. As the story went, Pappy knocked on the door at a bootleg joint, and when a man inside asked who was there, Pappy answered, "DeLoatch." The man thought Pappy said "the roach" and took him inside, where others broke his leg and cut his thumb off.

Pappy was the boyfriend of Janie Simon, Harriet Thornhill's sister, who shared the house with her.

Miss Harriet was noted for the nasality of her speech, which we referred to as "talking through her nose." She operated an elevator in Millner's Department Store downtown. Her twin sons, Hubert and Herbert, were about Noon's age. The other son, Tucker, an immaculate dresser, was about six years older than I. Clarence Thornhill, who was the only person other than Mr. McDaniel living on McKinley Street with a car, seemed to get a used General Motors car every other year.

This cliff is below the woods that bordered the DeLoatch house. Icicles formed as a result of the perpetual flow of water from the rocks. The base of the cliff ends at the northeast side of the Norfolk & Western railroad tunnel.

Earl DeLoatch was the most colorful person in this household. Known for his bebop caps worn askew and for communicating in nonsensical phrases, such as "studio on the Gordon," Earl, along with Clarence and Pappy, often sat on their front porch in metal lawn chairs, drinking Schlitz beer. This was the only house where I saw alcohol consumed in the open.

Paul and Morris Simon could claim two residences: they lived on Fifth Street between Taylor and Monroe and at 8 McKinley Street in the DeLoatch household. Miss Janie was Paul's favorite aunt, and when she died in the early 1950s, I could hear him mourning inside his home, while I sat on my porch. As I listened to Paul cry unabashedly, I felt the finality of death, though I wanted a Hollywood ending where Miss Janie would appear the next day to star in another role. My hope faded as I watched the wreath placed over the front door.

Morris and Paul's father, Paul, Sr., worked for Carl B. Hutcherson Funeral Home. Mr. Simon drove a 1946 Dynaflow Buick that could be recognized by its distinct sound as it approached the top of McKinley Street. I considered this Buick to be the most classic one of all until the box-shaped 1954 models appeared.

Paul had another brother, "Johnny Boy," who lived in Lovingston, about thirty miles away. When space was available, Mr. Simon, sensitive to our neighborhood bonds, occasionally would invite Billie and me to tag along to visit Johnny Boy in Lovingston. Since our family had no car, we eagerly jumped at any opportunity to ride in one.

The woods bordering our yard sloped down to a point just above the train tunnel. In contrast, the woods bordering the DeLoatch home ended on a rocky cliff fifty feet above the tracks.

Situated between our house and the DeLoatch house was a streetlight that stood in a line behind two huge sycamore trees. We had to rely on this single light, hidden from view, to illuminate the otherwise dark street until we walked about halfway up the hill. Whenever the streetlight burned out, I cautiously walked in the middle of the street in the dark, hoping to find my way by lights in our house.

When we first moved to McKinley Street, the Scott family, the largest one in the neighborhood, lived at 30 Federal Street on the corner of Federal and McKinley. Mr. and Mrs. Scott had seven girls: Helen, Gloria, Henrietta, Rebecca ("Becky"), Pamelia ("Daisy"), Sarah, and Theresa. Henry Elmo "Junie" Scott, Jr., one of my best friends, was the lone son, though he shared

This outdoor hydrant is all that remains of the house that was razed at 30 Federal Street.

space in the house with his nephew, Lafayette Silas "Stretch" Rose, Jr.

The Scotts moved to 171 McIvor Street shortly after we arrived on McKinley, and their prior residence at 30 Federal Street, the last house on the first block of Federal Street, adjacent to McKinley Street, was demolished. Sisters Anna and Jenny Wright lived at 28 Federal Street, while at 26 Federal lived the elderly Mrs. Blair, to whom Momma often provided altruistic caregiver services. A reluctant Billie accompanied Momma and had the responsibility of washing Mrs. Blair's hair.

Frank Hawkins lived in the next house at 24 Federal Street, previously occupied by Miss Elaine. The Anderson family lived in the first house on this first block at 22 Federal Street as it curved and morphed into McIvor Street. The Anderson family was comprised of mother Ruth, who worked as a cook at the hospital, and her children Willie, Gloria, and Catherine, who, even though much older than I, accepted me as their playmate.

Across the street, about twenty-five yards northeast of the railroad tunnel under Hollins Mill Road, stood the foundation of the house formerly occupied by John Tweedy, an African American. According to the 1938 City Directory, his address was 19 Federal Street, and his neighbor at 21 Federal Street was Thomas Jackson. Miss Elaine told me that their houses were destroyed to accommodate the widening of Hollins Mill Road. As pre-teens, we would often use the concrete foundation as a picnic area, and would eagerly await Spring so we could pick the daffodils that bloomed nearby.

The 1914 City Directory showed the first block of Federal Street beginning at Blackwater Creek and continuing to Norvell (McKinley) Street. By 1915, a portion of this block of Federal Street had become McIvor Street.

A patch of hostile blackberries grew in the teardrop-shaped plot where Federal Street yielded to McIvor Street and Hollins Mill Road. The only billboard erected on Tinbridge Hill divided the blackberries from the one-story Scott home, hidden behind ever-changing McBride's signs.

White families lived in the next three houses. A field of luscious dewberries as large as my thumb grew unclaimed and separated the whites from two more homes occupied by blacks. The last black family was the McCoys, who could count among their siblings Carroll, Robert, Rosamond, Mitchell, and Ersie, one of my soon-to-be classmates.

Next to the McCoys lived another white family, the Hammocks, whose boys, Mike and Kent, sometimes played with older black boys like my brothers. Mr. Trent lived in the next house, which was set deeper in the woods and, with a little stretch of the imagination, could be described as a cabin.

The last house on the street was in its own league. It was at the end of the McIvor Street cul-de-sac, and its architecture bordered on being a holdover from the neocolonial period. Stately columns, a spacious yard, and an attached garage that held a rare Packard defined this house as belonging to someone with money. An elderly white lady, Mrs. Isbell, and her husband, Harry, lived here, and black children rarely gathered enough nerve to venture to the house, located at the end of a long sidewalk in the fenced-in yard.

The yard contained a covered well that Junie said was rumored to extend to China. Although we doubted the veracity of this story, we made unsuccessful attempts to sneak into the yard to gauge for ourselves.

As McIvor Street made the return trip from the cul-de-sac, the terrain on the left side of the street yielded no room for houses. This pristine environment had pathways along the precarious ridge that we cautiously traversed. A misstep could lead to a death tumble along the rocky cliffs and massive trees.

The steepness of the ridge faded as the elevation of the street reached its peak across from the dewberry patch. The rubble of a shack marked one of many escape routes we could take to re-enter the street. Someone had thoughtfully placed a dirt spur line off the street to allow drivers an opportunity to turn around instead of driving down to the cul-de-sac.

Mrs. Clara DePriest, an elderly white lady who lived diagonally across from the Scotts, had a strawberry patch where an assortment of accomplices and I crawled through high grass to obtain off-limits fruit.

A grove of trees and a telephone easement gave way to the woods, where I took shortcuts to get to the backyards of my closest neighbors on Federal and McIvor streets. Twice these woods caught fire. The first time it happened, I was away exploring other parts of our community. Although the woods backed up to our yard, we were never in any imminent danger because the firefighters were quick to respond. I felt a loss of nature and privacy when I went in our backyard to view the smoldering remains of an area that had once supplied me with an exclusive entranceway to nature's local wonders. The woods, though, were resilient and the next spring rebounded with verdant growth, though some of the larger trees bore scars of the fire.

The second time the woods caught fire, I was again disappointed, but after witnessing the way they rebounded after the first fire, I hoped for a full recovery. No one ever found out who started the first fire, but years later Junie confessed that he had accidentally started the second one.

Thus ends the tour of the size and shape of the neighborhood that remains a part of me today.

New Friends and Neighbors

My new friendships on McKinley Street began when Billie introduced me to my across-the-street neighbor, Rowena Lois McDaniel, who was saddled with the mistaken nickname of "Moosecat," a corruption of "Pussycat." Rowena greeted me warmly and assumed the role of five-year-old hostess as she introduced me to Junie, who would become my closest friend.

Rowena's first order of business included playing "Guess His Name" with Junie. After tossing out a few common male names with no success, the exasperated Junie sized up my face and, looking at my runny nose, guessed "Snotty Nose." Rowena corrected him with a childlike rebuke as Rowena, Junie, and I forged the beginning of a lifetime bond. Other introductions to friends paled in comparison, but soon everybody in the neighborhood got to know the new kids on the block.

Paul Simon, who frequently stayed next door to us under the supervision of his beloved Aunt Janie, gave my oldest brother, Carl, his nickname. Since Carl was a "junior," we naturally called him "June" when we lived on Polk Street. But Paul was also a junior and called "June," resulting in a conflict. I guess Paul called squatter's rights and felt he had first dibs on the name. As he and the older group of boys gathered around my brother, Paul pointed out that my brother had a large head that looked like a moon, so he called him "Moon," which was close enough to June. However, as a compromise, Paul changed it to "Noon," which became my brother's permanent sobriquet.

Paul had a flair for colorful language, which contrasted sharply with my reticence. Some of the boys like Ronnie Douglas or Bill McDaniel challenged Paul to tone down his cussing, which blended effortlessly with every sentence or started each utterance from his lips. On the other hand, my vocabulary was so pristine that I used no profanity at all.

Paul's cousin, Tucker, was by far the neatest dresser in our circle of friends. He had the advantage of having a mother who worked in a downtown department store, a job that affected the quality and style of his clothes. Tucker was quite competitive, and, being several years older than I, often took advantage of my lack of coordination to defeat me in sports and games. I didn't mind too much because I liked having fun.

My brothers, Lafayette and Carl, stand in our yard. In the background, clothes from the DeLoatch house hang from a pulley clothesline. Houses on Rivermont Avenue are barely visible near the top left corner of the picture.

As I got older and my hand-eye coordination improved, my skills also increased, as Tucker discovered. He used to beat me regularly at horseshoes (referred to as "skunk heels" by a young Bumpsie) that we played in his back yard. The first time I beat him by topping one of his "fives," he realized that I posed a threat to his horseshoe supremacy and never played that game with me again.

William "Bill" McDaniel forged bonds with many of us younger boys, like Rand, Junie, and me—all the same age—and the slightly older Paul Simon and Mitchell McCoy. Bill took us on treks through the woods, exploring every nook and cranny of Blackwater Creek and the surrounding cliffs. With him we journeyed from the mouth of the creek that ended at the James River in the lower basin of Lynchburg, up to the Tate Springs Road site where the new Lynchburg General Hospital would be built in 1955.

Mitchell McCoy lived in the last house on McIvor Street that was occupied by blacks. The remaining houses held residents we identified, as we did most of the whites in our neighborhood, as poor white trash. The lone exception was the residents at the end of the McIvor Street cul-de-sac.

Mitchell compensated for his small stature with a toughness that reminded me of Audie Murphy, the most decorated World War II hero in America. No matter how hard I tried, I could not beat Mitchell in anything except for schoolwork, which he cared little about. The first time we engaged in physical play, I was about seven years old. In the McDaniels' spacious, sloping yard, he put me in a chokehold as part of a McKinley Street versus McIvor Street wrestling match.

As Mitchell squeezed harder, he asked me, "Do you give up?" My body and mind hadn't come to grips with the predicament I faced. Stubbornness numbed the chokehold, and I defiantly told Mitchell, "Nope." Determined to make me yield, he squeezed harder. I endured, telling myself, "This ain't hurting me."

He pressed on. Suddenly, my body and mind got in sync, communicating "This is not good." My body fought back in dramatic fashion and showed the mettle of my machismo: I threw up. Mitchell released his grip as a combination of tears and stomach contents spewed in full view of all my friends. I blathered all the way home, convulsing from defeat and seeking the comfort of Momma.

When Momma heard my story, she ruffled her maternal feathers and accosted Mitchell, who pleaded innocent because of my recalcitrance. His argument proved no match for Momma's defense of her last-born. She scolded him for his deed, then turned her attention toward me. She said I should have had enough sense to know when to quit. I maintained that Mitchell had caused me no pain, though tears and vomit contradicted my claim.

Mitchell lived like Herman Hesse's Narcissus. He played by his own rules, exploring life beyond our community and supplying the younger trio of Rand, Junie, and me with his more experienced perceptions of the world. He showed us how to make dice out of mud, how to detect crooked dice, and how to play the odds when betting. He talked about his relationships with the girls who fell under his charm. Whenever he returned from one of his adventures, he would give us a detailed description of what had

Randolph Austin, age twelve, sits on Wayne Scott's tricycle. Part of Mitchell McCoy is showing, and the DeLoatch home is behind the front hedges of the McDaniels' yard.

happened, leaving us to dream of what we could expect when we got older.

I considered Junie my best male friend growing up and Rowena my best female friend. Junie possessed a free spirit that contrasted with my extreme shyness, making us a prepubescent odd couple. He was handsome, outgoing, daring, and talented; I was homely and known for keeping my head down and mouth open. He generated mischief; I usually had to pay for it. From our first meeting, when he branded me "Snotty Nose," we complemented each other for years to come.

Rowena became my most intimate friend, living as she did right across the street and, like Junie, being my same age. She was the only friend in our community who started and completed school with me. Though nine months younger, she was definitely more precocious than I. We spent a lot of time at each other's houses, playing games, watching television, and completing homework assignments. Although I seldom said much, I sometimes found talking to her effortless once I got started.

When we played games, I often took unnecessary risks, trying to do things differently, while she had a steadier approach to playing and winning. My cockiness caused me to lose games that I could have easily won. When I went down in defeat, Rowena would advise me, on her road to victory, "Never take chances until you are sure of victory." It was a long time before I could apply this wisdom, but when I found myself on the losing end of sure things, her words would surface in my thoughts.

Three of Rowena's cousins stayed with Mr. and Mrs. Warren, her grandparents, beginning in the mid-1950s. Yvonne Bonet "Bonnie" Scott and her brothers, Wayne and Warren, moved from Washington, DC, with their mother, Cecilia. It took me a while to adjust to Bonnie's personality, which at first I found grating. As I got to know her, I became more tolerant and fond of this know-it-all girl, who was about three years my junior. Her brothers, much younger, were easier to get along with. Even though they were less mature, I accepted them into my play world.

I often tried to imagine myself as adopted by the McDaniel family because of the resources they had at their disposal. They had the largest yard in the neighborhood, and its slope invited us to play. We would position ourselves at the highest point of the yard, at the corner of the hedges that bordered the Field, and tumble head over heels until we reached the wire fence some fifty feet away. We varied our tumbling by shaping ourselves into human logs and rolling to our destination.

The McDaniels' yard offered a carefree and safe sanctuary. We played "throwing statues" and "ring around the roses" and made up other games as inspired. Our only fear was Rex, the McDaniels' unassuming spayed dog, who seldom did more than sleep and poop. It was the poop we feared more than anything. No one wanted to be identified as the person who stepped or rolled in dog "doo-doo." We developed good spatial skills thanks to Rex's

My sister Billie (left) and I were posing for this picture when Bonnie Scott, over my objections, asked Aunt Julia, who was the photographer, if she could join us. The disdain in my face would later yield to a strong friendship.

indiscriminate use of the yard as her bathroom.

For a long time a 1947 Plymouth was the McDaniels' family car, and, like Mr. Simon, Mr. McDaniel sometimes included Billie and me on excursions. Other times, when I saw them loading up for a visit, I longed to go with them but understood that I could not be included in all of their family outings.

I questioned Momma about Daddy's lack of transportation and found out that he used to have a truck but got rid of it. Living and working in Washington and traveling home maybe once a month justified Daddy's not owning a car. I adjusted to and accepted not ever seeing him behind the wheel of any vehicle.

Our excursions with different neighbors involved more than car rides. In the summers, groups of neighbors including the Scotts, McDaniels, and Andersons, banded together, washed out gallon-sized pails, trekked down Hollins Mill Road, crossed the bridge, and invaded Blackwater Street. Our goal was to pick every ripened blackberry off these plants that lined the hillside bordering the street. I don't know if groups from Rivermont objected to our tradition, since technically we were in their neighborhood. I never heard of any turf conflicts, and I never saw anyone other than us pick the berries.

As an eight- or nine-year old, I picked more slowly than some of the others, and when it seemed I might come up short in filling my bucket, one of the adults would pour a few blackberries into my container to help me reach my goal. These outings reinforced our neighborhood's cooperative spirit and passed it on to us younger ones. We practiced what we saw and developed strong ties as a result.

In the summer of 1955, the Johnson household gained a new member who would become a temporary friend. This friend left me with a lasting memory. Skeeter, whom I called "Skip," was a nephew of Miss Elaine's and had moved to Lynchburg from Philadelphia. I immediately took a liking to him, and his being a few months older than I made him an ideal playmate.

Skip was the first person my age who lived outside of Lynchburg that I ever befriended. He was easy to get along with, and I felt it was my social responsibility to introduce him to my other friends. Because he lived so close, I spent a disproportionate amount of playtime with him.

I looked forward to our being in the fifth grade together, but he told me that in all likelihood he would be put back a grade. Yet my hope of our being in the same grade ran high, until reality struck in September. I was promoted to the fifth grade, and he, as predicted, entered Mrs. Payne's fourth-grade class. We lost an opportunity for further bonding, and soon he announced that he was moving back to Philadelphia.

Nothing about our friendship was remarkable except that it was unpretentious. I had accepted him as an ideal playmate, meaning that whatever faults he had, I overlooked. We never had any tension, and I never felt the need to be competitive or domineering, even though I knew from our physical play and academic skills that I had a slight edge on him. His moving left a void in my friendships, though he probably never realized the impact he had on my life.

As I entered my early teens, I maintained a Peter Pan relationship with "Bud" Johnson, who was about seven years younger. We would play in my yard, where I often tried to awe him with my limited worldly skills. One day I tried unsuccessfully to dazzle him with rudimentary magic tricks, but he soon caught on to all my stunts. Then, out of the blue, I performed an unscripted trick that baffled him and, he says, still does. I asked him for a penny and let him examine it. Then I took the penny and threw it into the woods. After the penny sailed out of sight, I pulled it from behind his ear. He looked at me incredulously and said, "Let me see that penny." When he examined it, he saw that it had the same date as the one I threw and remained dumbfounded as to how I could have retrieved the coin. In deference to magicians everywhere, the solution to my trick will remain a secret.

Rowena had cousins from Rivermont who occasionally visited the McDaniel family. The Richardson children—John D., Carolyn, Christine, and Dennis—sometimes found time to include me in their activities. Knowing them expanded the world of friends with whom I re-connected once I began attending high school.

In the summer of 1956, two cousins, Gary Kirkland and his younger sister, Lucille, arrived from Arlington County to spend a week with us. My Aunt Dorothy had adopted and spoiled these children, whom we took in as part of our extended family. Gary was my age, though I was officially older by a few months. We looked so much alike that we were mistaken for brothers. This was a compliment to me; I took pleasure in being compared to someone who had an outgoing personality. Although we played well together, it would take a while before Billie and I convinced Momma that

Gary is on the right as we stand near the sidewalk beside the Warren fence. Miss Elaine's house is to the left.

while she thought that Gary was an ideal guest, he was manipulative. His antics did not dampen our relationship, and in exchange for his visit, I got to stay a week in Arlington.

When I went to Arlington, I thought I had been transplanted to the Deep South as depicted in the movie *Bright Road*. Aunt Dorothy lived with her husband, Uncle Curtis, on North Nineteenth Road. A few blocks to the north of their house stood a country store on a dirt road. Just like in the movies, someone sat on the wooden storefront porch whittling. This scene seemed far removed from cosmopolitan Washington, DC, only seven miles north.

My weeklong stay with Gary stretched out for an additional ten days after a local dog bit me while I was riding Gary's bike. The dog, a black terrier, had a reputation for barking and chasing children on bikes, but I think my being a newcomer gave it justification to sink its fangs into my leg. After I got patched up, I cruised the neighborhood on that bike, trying to get revenge. No matter how many times I pedaled near the dog's home, it would not take the bait. I was under rabies watch for ten days without ever getting retribution. Then I left Arlington and never returned.

My list of friends from the DeLoatch family increased when Elvis DeLoatch, who hailed from Washington, DC, moved in next door, accompanied by his family. Phyllis, who was my age, Elvis, Jr., Lloyd, and Casper brought life to the DeLoatch clan and me, now that my older playmates, the Thornhills and Simons, had moved on. Although the boys were much younger than I, we often played together without consideration of our age differences.

A rare group photo of friends. Front row: Theresa Scott, Hilda Rucker, Gloria Wright, Gail Rucker; second row: Lillian Austin, Richard Wright, Larry Rucker, Hugh Wright; last row: me, unidentified, Rowena McDaniel, unidentified

Dog Eat Dog and
Other Animals

Everyone on McKinley Street had animals. Although cats and dogs were prevalent, a relaxed animal code made possible the inclusion of other domesticated animals without controversy. Miss Elaine raised bantam chickens that lived in a chicken coop in her yard. Momma sometimes bought a chicken that she allowed to fatten in our yard before it became a Sunday meal.

Mr. McDaniel had a hog pen situated on the slope behind his fenced-in yard. Although I often sneaked through the woods to peek at the hogs, I never saw any of them get slaughtered. Children my age were discouraged from witnessing these events, but I could hear the death squeals from my yard.

During the spring of 1956 a wren flew through the lattice framework of our back porch and deposited a twig in Momma's clothespin basket, which was hanging inside the enclosed wall. The wren returned repeatedly, and I watched her nest grow as she left to select more building materials. Soon she sat in the nest and deposited four small turquoise eggs.

Because I watched this act of nature from the beginning, I took some ownership of the destiny that I was sure would ensue. In the summer I finally heard the peeps of the naked chicks as their featherless bodies cried for food.

The mother tried in vain to share food with them evenly, but one always seemed to be left out. I wanted to make adjustments to the food distribution to ensure the survival of all the chicks because I could see the neglected one weakening, but I had no power to interfere with this survival of the fittest and resigned myself to letting nature take its course. The weak chick finally died, and I believe I was the only organism saddened by the event.

The other chicks grew hardy and developed feathers as they approached flight age. I looked forward to being on hand for their inaugural flight; however, I was not alone. Pappy DeLoatch's cat marked them as easy prey and patrolled outside in our backyard, patiently awaiting the outcome of the chicks' first flight.

I expected some sort of warning from nature to alert me about the chicks' departure from their nest. Instead, I got a shock when, on that fateful day, I walked up the stairs to the back porch just as the chicks took flight. I knew the cat was standing motionless, ready for the attack, and I was prepared to defend my newly adopted family.

My plans went awry when one of the birds flew into our commode as the others flapped through the lattice, crashing to the ground. I was facing "Sophie's choice"—save the chick drowning in the toilet or monitor the progress of the other two chicks. While watching the two chicks descend to the ground from their flight burst, I ran to the toilet to retrieve the drowning chick.

Less than five seconds had elapsed since their departure from the nest. In that brief moment, I had not been swift enough to snatch the struggling chick from the toilet before it succumbed. I laid the dying chick on the porch and ran to the steps to check on the status of the other two. When I opened the screen door, I saw that the cat had slaughtered both chicks. Angrily I shooed the cat away, only to see the lifeless birds half-hidden in the grass.

I looked stoically at the carcasses. While in their nest they had been safe from harm; now they had paid the ultimate price for nature's call of the wild. The next year the mother wren returned to build another nest. This time I discarded her first few twigs from the clothespin basket, forcing her to build somewhere out of my sight so she and I would not have to go through another ordeal that summer.

With the exception of Ms. McIvor, every McKinley Street household had a dog. Miss Elaine owned an old wire-haired black and white terrier named Joe, who would bite me when I let my guard down but disappeared when I armed myself with rocks.

Joe's biggest claim to fame was killing one of two feral kittens, the offspring of the domesticated cat that belonged to the DeLoatches. The mother cat had birthed and raised these kittens in the woods, alienated from human contact. Sometimes they would come into my yard, where I tried to catch and pet them, only to be scratched and bitten for my efforts.

The kittens had roamed into Ms. McIvor's front yard when Joe, who had been monitoring their activities, trapped them by the porch wall. One kitten managed to escape as I tried to rescue the other one. Before I could jump the fence to force Joe to release his prey, he had snatched it by the scruff of the neck. With a couple of violent shakes, the kitten fell lifeless to the ground.

I picked up some rocks to avenge the death of this helpless animal, but Joe darted home before I could get to him. For the first time in my life, I had seen one animal kill another just for the sport of it. This brutal act reminded me of a cold reality about life and death. I almost ached with sadness when I saw this innocent creature, one that had tried to live in the wild, meet its fate in the jaws of a house pet.

Besides cats, the DeLoatch family had a black and white collie, Tony, who had to be chained because of his reputation for biting people. Whenever Tony escaped, neighbors reacted as though a rabid animal had invaded the community. They stayed inside and peered through windows as Tony ran rampantly through the neighborhood. Predictably, Tony would find an unsuspecting victim to bite before Paul or someone else from the DeLoatch family corralled him and returned him to his dog pen.

Contrasting with Tony's wild streak was Rex, the spayed brown dog of mixed lineage that belonged to the McDaniels. Rex's main functions were to eat, sleep, pant heavily in the summer, and dig holes under the hedges bordering her master's yard. She was the first dog I knew that could not bear puppies, making me wonder if she ever longed for a litter.

Ironically, the Warrens, the parents of Mrs. McDaniel, owned a dog named King, which made more sense to me than having a female dog named Rex, which I knew was Latin for "king."

Our family started a dog saga beginning with Princess, a cute cocker spaniel that was a gift from Cutchie's friend Hubert Paine, who lived at Fourth and Polk streets. Hubert had assured Momma that Princess was spayed, but in a few months I watched her give birth to a litter of puppies. I listened to Princess wail as Momma gave away all the puppies except one. Then Princess met the same fate as her puppies.

We named our puppy "Champ" and watched it grow a luxurious coat of hair. Someone told Momma that if she cut off all of Champ's hair, it would grow back even more magnificent. My mild protest drew little consideration as both layers of dog hair fell at Champ's feet. Soon he looked more like a newborn rodent than a six-week-old pup.

What Momma did not know was that dogs need their down hair for protection and temperature regulation. This fact became apparent when Champ came down with distemper. Life slowly and miserably ebbed out of him, leaving me without the first dog I could claim as my own.

About a year later we got a lovable Airedale I named Champ II, who became my trusted companion. Everywhere I went, Champ would dutifully and silently follow. We made quite a team as I paraded around in a coonskin cap Momma had made out of an old fox fur, and he accompanied me looking like a miniature albino sheepdog. Champ was loyal and smart, although my dog-training expertise stopped at "fetch."

I never thought Champ would be much of a fighter, considering he was as mild-mannered as I was and an Airedale, a breed not known to strike fear in the hearts of other dogs. My perception of Champ changed when he came face to face with the Douglas's dog, Teddy, who had a reputation for being territorial, if not tough.

Champ and I were walking home when we arrived at the steps of the Douglas house. Teddy came out, and the two dogs began sniffing each other. Fearing the worst, I called Champ, but before I could get a response, the two dogs squared off. To my surprise, Champ stood toe-to-toe with Teddy and backed him down. Teddy retreated, and Champ came to me as if nothing had happened. I stroked and petted him as if he had won the dogfight of the century. I couldn't wait to tell my friends about my feisty dog.

One of Champ's more memorable escapades provided a source of community amusement and embarrassment, plus, for me, a short lesson on the birds and bees. Champ had rumbled through the neighborhood garbage cans and stumbled upon a toy that sent him into euphoria: a discarded sanitary pad. Much like a cat with a catnip bag, he tossed the pad in the air as he ran around the Field. Then he would muzzle his nose in it as if he were snorting cocaine. Blushing neighbors watched, but no one made an effort to remove Champ's "toy" from his grasp. I was too naïve to understand what was happening, so after hearing whispers about the object that made Champ reach another level of consciousness, I asked the worldly Mitchell, "What's a Kotex?" He responded in graphic words I dare not repeat. But in one sentence, he taught me another difference between boys and girls.

As soon as I became accustomed to Champ as a lifelong pet, tragedy struck. On a Saturday in the late spring of 1955, Champ, after one of his romps through the neighborhood, ran into our back yard yelping so loudly in pain that it alarmed the whole neighborhood. He started running in swooping circles howling in agony and foaming at the mouth as neighbors congregated in our yard to watch this curious sight.

We stood around trying to guess what was happening. Although he foamed at the mouth, we ruled out rabies, knowing this spell had come on too suddenly to be that disease. Soon, Champ, exhausted, fell to the ground, moaning and breathing heavily as I watched helplessly along with the others. Finally his breathing subsided, and I saw him take his last gasp of air as he closed his eyes.

We all inched closer, concluding, for lack of any other explanation, that he must have had a fit. Though I didn't shed any tears, my heart was heavy because I had to witness my dog suffer unimaginable agony and die before he reached the peak of his life. The gap he left in my young life reminded me of the fragility of life and finality of death.

My memory of Champ ends with the image of his final moments. I have no recollection of how we disposed of his body. I do recall that we opted not to bury him in our yard, but nothing comes to mind after that. I guess the blocking of the memory of Champ's disposal was nature's way of adjusting a ten-year-old brain to the cycle of life.

The following Monday when I went to school, I told my fourth-grade teacher, Ms. Jones, of my loss, and she suggested that I relay my story to the rest of the class. I assumed she felt my telling the story would be cathartic and help bring closure to my tragedy, but my version of the events didn't have the air of seriousness that I tried to convey. When I concluded with deadpan affect that Champ had died as a result of a fit, it brought snickers from my classmates.

When I arrived home from school, Momma gave me a more plausible explanation of Champ's death. Mr. Josh, the jovial cook at the hospital, told her that he had recently put down some rat poison around the building and Champ might have eaten some of it. This could explain the foaming and Champ's quick death. I accepted this explanation and felt better knowing what had possibly happened. I could not blame anyone for the tragedy, though I wished there was some way it could have been avoided and I could have had Champ back.

Champ, the summer before being poisoned

About two years later, we received a puppy from one of Momma's friends. Princess, a mixed tri-colored shepherd, offered me consolation for Champ. Our choice of names illustrated our lack of creativity; however, Princess was a pretty dog, distinguished by the white diamond on her forehead and white paws that made her seem to prance as she walked.

Momma didn't want a repeat of the history of our first Princess, so she got Princess II spayed. One of my duties was to make sure that Princess healed according to the instructions of Dr. Dictor, our veterinarian. I guarded against her removing the bandage on her shaved abdomen and replaced it whenever it came loose.

Although the surgery was successful, Princess never fully recovered. She developed distemper, and her nervous system began to break down. I became her primary caregiver, wiping the crusts that formed daily around her eyes and cleaning the green slime that exuded from her nostrils.

Dr. Dictor gave us some pills that I had to administer daily. Trying to get Princess to swallow her medicine tested my patience, because this was an unnatural act for her. Often she would slip the pill to the side of her mouth and spit it out when she got the opportunity. Ever vigilant, I would watch for signs that she had refused to swallow, then gently wrap one hand around her snout while stroking her throat. I often had to repeat this routine several times before achieving a measure of success. I wished she understood that this medicine was for her own good, which added to the frustration of this experience.

The pills helped somewhat, but I noticed that Princess had developed a twitch in her right rear leg. She moved it as if she were beginning to scratch her tummy, but never completed the act. This infrequent act soon appeared with alarming regularity, and I had to take her back to Dr. Dictor, who gave me more pills.

Even with the pills, her condition deteriorated, and soon she lost mobility in that leg as the other hind one developed the same symptom. Eventually both legs became paralyzed. Now I was faced with seeing the demise of another pet.

Our budget was being stressed, and I had to take Princess back to see Dr. Dictor. Momma could afford to get me a taxi to the animal hospital, but I had to make the mile-long return trip on foot.

I scooped up Princess, who weighed about thirty pounds and wore a leash, and walked about two blocks before I began to tire. I rested, while Princess valiantly tried to walk, dragging her hind legs. Regaining my strength, I picked her up again. Each time I repeated this process, the distance between my rest stops became shorter as my muscles began to burn. Soon tears began to well up in my eyes because this ordeal was taxing both my strength and my emotions.

I knew Princess suffered, and I could not relieve her misery. I kept looking for a good Samaritan to drive by and take me home but concluded that nobody would want to take a chance on giving me a ride with a dog as sick as Princess.

I reached Fifth and Federal streets, which I estimated was a halfway point. "Only eight more blocks to go," I told myself. I gathered up my strength and resolved to make one final push with Princess in my arms. I carried her to the middle of the block between Fourth and Third, near the Stalling tobacco warehouse, when my arms, despite my best efforts, melted like butter.

We had just passed the warehouse when I decided to put her down again. Princess, sensing familiar territory, did not rest. She struggled on, as I held her leash. At that moment, two teenaged girls, who were walking in the opposite direction on the other side of the street, spotted me.

Soon after they passed the house of my future history teacher, Mrs. Womack, one of them said, sympathetically, "Aww, look at that dog." And with outrage, the other one said, "That boy ought to be ashamed of himself for making that dog walk like that. He ought to be whipped."

Those words pierced my heart. I wanted to shout across the street to let them know what I had been through. If only they could have experienced the pain that I felt, if only they could have walked in my shoes, then they might have spoken with empathy for me as well as my dog.

I continued to carry Princess, wishing her suffering would end. Never before had I wished that death would come to an animal, but with no visible signs of improvement, what else could I wish for?

We finally made it home, and Princess began to waste away. Through it all, Princess had a sort of Pollyanna look about her, as if to tell me, "Don't worry, death isn't so bad."

Princess died shortly after our visit to the vet, and my heart filled with sadness and relief. As with the death of Champ, I have no memory of how we disposed of her remains. I know we had no type of dog funeral or memorial. Death must leave a gap in my memory for a reason I have yet to figure out.

Miss Elaine acquired another dog to replace Joe, whose death from old age I secretly celebrated. She now owned a full-grown female boxer that attracted packs of male dogs of all breeds when she went into heat. I watched dogs large and small fight each other for the chance to extend their bloodlines. One little chihuahua could reach only to the boxer's back leg and humped that, while other dogs were more successful.

Momma was given one of the offspring, which she passed on to me.

I persuade Drac to pose for Aunt Julia. The McDaniel home is to the right. In the faint background above my head is the dome of Jones Memorial Library.

Once again, I lacked creativity in naming the pup, so Momma proposed "Dracula." I thought, "Great. Another awkward name for me to deal with." I assented, and Dracula became our first dog to bear a nickname, "Drac."

Although Drac was mixed, he had most of the features of a purebred boxer, minus the droopy jowls. Momma decided to make Drac fit the image of a show dog by getting his ears trimmed and tail clipped. Once again, I issued a mild protest, but Momma had the upper hand. When Drac was about six months old, we took a trip to the animal hospital to have the cosmetic surgery done.

I tended to his bandages, which irritated him and caused a bit of sadness in me, knowing that he probably was confused about losing his body parts. I don't know if the surgery had any effect on his personality, but soon Drac began to stray from home.

The first time Drac left, I thought I'd never see him again. Then one day I was walking down McIvor Street past Mitchell's house when I saw Drac in the yard of the white family next door. I went up to the fence, where two brothers, Mike and Kent, were standing, and told them they had my dog. The brothers, who sometimes played with some of the older black boys, told me that they had found Drac, but they put up no protest about my claim and returned my dog without incident. Drac seemed happy to see me and indifferent about leaving the brothers. I embraced him around his collarless neck; then we walked home together. We bought another collar and an identification tag just in case he ran away again.

He stayed with us for a few more months before straying once more. I searched his usual haunts but after a while lost all hope of ever seeing him again. Then one day James Norfleet told me he had seen Drac in the yard of one of the notorious bootleggers near the Black Bottom. He lived near the corner of Third and Jackson streets, just below the house where my older schoolmates, Louise Powell and her younger sister, Sandra, lived.

Hope sprang forward in my mind as I walked to the house of the man to whom I had once sold dandelions that would be converted into bootleg wine. I saw Drac, and my heart started racing. I approached the man, who was around forty-five, and told him that he had my dog.

My anticipation of reuniting with Drac was

Drac sits in the McDaniels' yard, while Wayne Scott looks on. Our home is directly behind him, and his home is to the left of ours.

crushed when the man asked, "Do you have any proof that this is your dog?" His question let me know immediately that he had a covetous nature. I told him that I knew my dog when I saw him. He responded, "I don't see no collar on him." I explained how he lost collars. "You ain't got no proof, then you don't get the dog." Frustrated, and unable to use force, I walked away trying to figure out a strategy as I watched this heartless man load Drac into the trunk of his 1952 Chevrolet.

I told Momma of my discovery, and though she was in my corner, she let me try to figure it out. I returned to the bootlegger's house without a game plan, though I had considered reporting the incident to the police. When I arrived at his house, I found no trace of him, his car, or Drac. I was told later that he had taken Drac to rural Gladys, Virginia. I never saw Drac again.

For months I would walk by the bootlegger's house, hoping to find that Drac had returned, but he never did. Each time I saw the bootlegger, I gave him the most contemptuous look my fourteen-year-old face could muster. I had lost all respect for him for taking advantage of me and wished misfortune and ill health on him for the rest of his life.

The final dog that we got before moving off McKinley Street was a small terrier, Ricky, that was successfully spayed. Again, I don't know if this operation affected her temperament, but she was feisty and territorial. By now, I had become cautious about bonding too closely with dogs, although she lived longer than all our other dogs combined.

Accidents Do Happen

Acquiring scars is an unwritten rite of passage for boys. About a year after moving to McKinley Street, I began to accumulate an assortment of wounds to add to my existing collection of identifying marks.

Hollins Mill Road played a prominent role in my first neighborhood accident. I had accompanied Bill, Junie, and Rand across the Hollins Mill bridge. Thanks to Aunt Julia, who lived in Garden City, New York, and worked as a domestic, I was wearing corduroy knickerbockers, out of style by about a generation. I was the only boy in my neighborhood whose pants played music as he walked.

A stream flowed from the Rivermont side of Hollins Mill Road and emptied into Blackwater Creek. Bill led us across this stream so we could get closer to the dam. Junie and Rand successfully navigated the rocks in the water, but when I attempted to cross, the first rock I stepped on was covered with moss. This type of rock, I found out moments later, was called "slick rock." Had I found out sooner, my foot might not have come out from under me as I fell face first into the water. My mouth reluctantly embraced one of the rocks, causing blood to ooze from between my front teeth, and my knickerbockers soaked up water like a sponge as I considered the consequences I faced if I went home wet.

As I thought about facing Momma, I blubbered like the seven-year-old I was. Bill and the others consoled me by taking me to the other side of the bridge, where we took turns jumping into the sand below. Gradually I felt better, although the sand added to the weight of the wet corduroy. Soon my pants dried enough for me to go home without any evidence of my first disaster. Fortunately, my wound was not noticeable except in my mind, where I questioned why I was the one who had to fall. Little did I know that I would lead the neighborhood in experiencing minor calamities.

My first lasting McKinley Street wound came as I allowed my seven-year-old ego to give way to Lillian Smith, who was about four years older. Momma had bought me a second-hand bicycle, a red Roadmaster that I had barely mastered balancing, when Lillian, who lived with Miss Elaine, approached me. I stood at the top of the hill facing Federal Street when she asked, "Do you know how to ride?"

"Unh huh." I definitely was not going to embarrass myself by acknowledging I couldn't ride my bike.

"Can you double?"

"Unh huh."

"Can you take me down the hill?"

"Unh huh."

Lillian climbed on while I tried to steady my bike as I prepared for our McKinley Street descent.

Before continuing with this story, let me give you some background that will factor heavily into this incident.

In the summer, going barefooted was as acceptable as wearing shoes. I was on my bike, shoeless, and I was about to embark on a journey—riding down a hill, which I had never done before, with someone sitting behind me—another first—without knowledge of how to use brakes. There I was, trying to impress someone, yet without the skills necessary to do so.

I had total disregard for my safety and Lillian's as I pumped my bike down the hill. As I got closer to Federal Street, I realized that we were on a collision course with death. I panicked and, not knowing how to apply brakes, prepared to stop by any means necessary. When I got to the bottom of the hill, I turned my wheels sharply toward McIvor Street, causing the bike to slide in the gravel.

A disheveled Lillian dusted off the dirt and rock as she regained her composure, saying, "Are you all right? I thought you knew how to ride."

"I'm all right," I lied, concentrating on the two deep scrapes on the top of my right foot. Without a further word, I rescued my bike and hauled it up the hill, with Lillian accompanying me. Lillian peeled off to her house, while I limped home with the bicycle in tow.

Using the classic behavior of a young boy in shock, I waited until I saw Momma's face before wailing at the top of my lungs, releasing the pent-up pain. She cleaned my wound with gentian violet as my boohooing subsided.

"How did you make it all the way home before you started crying?" she asked. Between sniffles, I wondered about this myself. I was just glad she was there when I needed her.

For the rest of the summer I had to go barefooted or wear sandals, which I dreaded. My main focus was keeping flies off the sore as the iridescent purple stuff worked its healing magic. The two ugly circular scars that formed caused me to be self-conscious about showing my feet in public. Lillian would be the first and last girl that I doubled on my bike.

My next notable scar came as I played with the usual group—Bill, Junie, and Rand—on one of the ridges off McIvor Street. We were sliding down one of the steep pathways when I collided with an outcropping of rock that left an inch-and-a-half scar on my left shin. Though it was not an agonizing wound, it was deep enough to be a permanent reminder of the dangers of our domain.

Another wound came from a swarm of wasps that attacked me a few years later. I had experienced a bee sting before, when I was about eight. I was trying to imitate Junie, who said he had captured a bumblebee by entrapping it in a hibiscus flower. My attempt backfired when my prey began to back out of the flower as I closed the petals. For the first time in my life, my thumb felt like it had been hit with an electric current. I snatched my hand back and ran to the spigot, dousing it with water to minimize the throbbing.

That bee incident was a forerunner to the wasp attack. Wasps had begun building a nest at the corner of the screen door on our back porch. We had destroyed many such nests that had blossomed around the gutters and other areas of our house, so the wasps' presence was not intimidating.

I had been stung by a single wasp before, but this time I was in for a full assault. I had climbed the steps to our back porch and let the screen door slam behind me. When I did, the shock rattled the nest, and three wasps pounced on me. One attacked my left forearm and one my right, while the third landed on my head. It seemed they stung in unison as I flailed, brushing one off my head and another off my right forearm. While I concentrated on getting those two off me, the other wasp inflicted more damage on my left arm. As I turned to get rid of him, I noticed that not only do wasps sting, they bite. Before the wasp could make a full meal of my arm, I smashed it, sending it from my arm to wasp heaven.

Afterward I ran up to my room and fell across the bed, moaning like a wounded animal. No one was home to nurse my wounds, so I suffered alone. Exhausted, I looked at the lumps on my arm and felt the one on my head and then fell asleep. Once I awoke, I returned to the scene of the attack, armed with a Flit can filled with insecticide, and vanquished my enemy while unknowingly polluting the air with DDT.

It would be years before another childhood injury would leave a mark upon my flesh. In 1959, Lynchburg received a significant amount of snow that caused some of the streets on Tinbridge Hill to be closed to traffic. Our lack of sleighs failed to deter us from taking advantage of Polk Street hill. We crafted sleds out of cardboard boxes or anything that could slide on snow.

On this particular day, we had worn through several sheets of cardboard when Lee Stevens and a few other boys appeared with the mother of all makeshift sleds: a car hood appropriated from the Dickerson Buick car lot, located a few blocks away. We stood in awe as Lee and the other boys tugged that monolithic piece of sheet metal to the corner of Third and Polk streets. We visualized an unbridled descent that bottomed out at Second Street, over fifty feet below.

Impetuous as any fifteen-year-old, I hopped on the hood first; then others piled on top of me. All of a sudden, I realized that I had no control of this adventure. With all the weight on me, I was unable to grip any part of the hood. We had no way to steer the hood, which never reached the bottom of the hill. Our thrill ride ended soon after we passed the towering tulip tree, where we rammed into a huge bank of snow. Bodies flew everywhere, but no one appeared to be hurt. I only felt bruised until I saw the deep gash in my new car coat, which foretold an injury more serious than a bump.

Although I was not bleeding, I looked at a deep J-shaped cut on my right elbow. I took off my coat to examine the damage more closely and noticed the razor-sharp slice near the right scapula region of my garment. The guys gathered around emoting "oohs" of sympathy as I painfully put my coat back over the gash in my shoulder, which I could barely see.

Unassisted, I walked home, where Billie had piled dishes in our dishpan in anticipation of my completing one of the chores I had neglected to do. The delight she expected at seeing me was shortchanged when I said, as I pulled off my coat, "I don't think I'll be able to do the dishes today." Alarm replaced glee as Billie got in touch with my mother, who was working at the hospital.

When I arrived at the emergency room, a compassionate white doctor examined my arm and asked me to move my fingers, wanting assurance that I had suffered no nerve damage. I wiggled my fingers to his satisfaction, and he said that if the wound had been a little deeper, I could have lost the use of some of my fingers.

He loaded my wounds with Novocain, but evidently not enough, because when he clipped what I thought was dead or deadened skin, pain shot immediately to my brain.

"Did you feel that?" he asked. "Yeah," I said, rather indignantly. The doctor gave me another shot of Novocain and sewed three stitches in my elbow. Then he turned his attention to the gash near my right scapula. Once again, my imperviousness to Novocain caused me to wince in pain. This time I gripped the gurney on which I lay and endured getting three more stitches.

The next day I went to school, showing my bandaged arm to my friends from beneath my long-sleeved flannel shirt and preparing to eat some foolish words. At lunch, I was sitting at a table with some of the guys who had witnessed my accident. I mentioned to them that whoever touched my arm was going to be in for some trouble. As soon as these words left my lips, John Minnis walked by, greeting me with a warm hello and a tap on my injured arm. Immediately I jumped up with fire in my eyes.

John looked puzzled, trying to figure out what my problem was. As fast as I jumped up, I came to my senses, realizing that he had no idea of my injury and that for me to consider retaliation for his saying hello to me was foolish. With humility I backed away and let him know he had done nothing wrong. Then I sat down, recalibrating my ego, knowing that I still had some growing to do.

Fruit of the Limbs

Our neighborhood contained a modest variety of fruit trees and berries. With the exception of the Johnson household, every yard on McKinley Street bore some kind of fruit. When we moved onto the street, we were rewarded with an aging black-heart cherry tree in the throes of its last fruit-bearing season. On the edge of our back yard, just before the woods took over, stood a bountiful apple tree that yielded some of the tastiest apples my young palate had ever experienced. In the summer of 1953, I ate twenty-one apples in one day, which I later paid for with a short burst of "the runs."

In November of the following year, dependency on this source of nutrition and pleasure came to an end when Hurricane Hazel uprooted the apple tree as I watched from our kitchen window. After the storm had passed, I inspected the damage and concluded that the tree, though prone on the ground, could reattach itself and bear fruit.

I tried to push the tree back up but discovered that it was much heavier than I had imagined. The only way I could even budge the tree was to jump on its prone trunk, an action that had no bearing on my goal. I hoped a miracle would allow the tree to adjust to its new position and re-root in the fertile soil, but my ray of hope for another season of apples faded when the tree failed to blossom the following spring. I had the task of cutting up the tree for firewood, a sorrowful end to such a bountiful tree.

A wild cherry tree grew at the corner of Pappy DeLoatch's yard and ours. No one claimed ownership of the tree, and I was the only one who cared about climbing it to get the pea-sized fruits.

My sister Billie and I climb the branchless black-heart cherry tree. The woods behind us slope to the train tunnel about fifty feet below. In the far background to the right is Rivermont.

The wild cherry tree served a dual function: it supplied me both fruit and entertainment. Several thick vines snaked their way through the top branches. I cut one near its base and swung over the terrain between our yard and the DeLoatches'. My airborne thrill ended when the vine snapped, sending me abruptly, though safely, into the bushes, a few feet below.

I gathered my wits and thought about Sonny Brooks, who had experienced a far more dangerous spill. Looking up at the wild cherry tree, I decided that it had outlived its usefulness. And at the tender age of eleven I decided to reenact my version of the George Washington myth. I went under our crawl space, picked up our small ax, and began chipping away at the huge cherry tree.

It took what seemed like an eternity for me to accomplish my goal, but, like a rat nibbling on cheese, I finally delivered the coup de grace, and the tree fell towards the woods near the cliffs in back of the DeLoatches' yard.

My renewed pride transformed me from George Washington into Paul Bunyan. Having conquered forest flora, I stood on the vanquished tree and suddenly realized: "I am the idiot peasant who killed the goose that laid the golden egg." I had destroyed a perfectly good tree that had done me no harm.

Now that my stupidity was revealed, I had more work to do. This tree would be chopped up for firewood, and I hoped that the flames of our Warm Morning would release the wood's sweet smell. This never happened. All I got out of this sacrificial tree was ashes of remorse from knowing I had performed a useless act against nature.

The DeLoatches owned two Bartlett pear trees that grew from the base of the hillside that also served as their refuse site. The most luscious pears dangled on limbs impossible to reach. When the pears ripened, the yellow jackets would get first dibs, rendering the choicest fruit the domain of the most feared insect in the area. By the time I scavenged these fallen fruits, they were unsuitable for human consumption.

I tried to compensate by throwing rocks or sticks at the hanging fruit but usually wound up knocking huge chunks out of the pears of my desire before I could dislodge them from their stems.

Mr. McDaniel had two peach trees that produced two different varieties of fruit. Usually the trees were off-limits, but on rare occasions, I had opportunities to climb and pick some of the leftovers.

Mr. Warren had pears and grapes, neither of which I was able to enjoy. The grapes were temptingly close to his fence, but I couldn't squeeze my arm far enough through the fence to touch the vines. I would take the path that ran the length of our backyard to McIvor Street and try to climb his fence for the pears, which was protected by his dog, King. My fear of King kept those pears from within my reach, so I settled on daring raids to the plum trees of Ms. McIvor. I probably could have had more success at getting her plums had I asked. I was too scared to ask, but not too scared to sacrifice my body to Momma's switches in case she found out about my theft.

A path at the edge of our yard connected to other wooded paths that emerged at the beginning of McIvor Street. One of these paths bordered the Anderson house at 22 Federal Street, where a mulberry tree bore an abundance of fruit. I used to eat mulberries until my hands and mouth turned purple. Then one day I decided to take some home and combine them with my morning cereal. This would be the last time I ate mulberries.

Since I knew that small bugs lurked within each piece of fruit—I would blow them off before eating the berries—I concluded that if I washed and soaked mulberries in water, the bugs would drown. Then I could put them on my corn flakes. My strategy failed; the golden urchins floated in my milk like inner tubes at Jefferson Park Pool. Irritated and dismayed, I submerged another batch of mulberries beneath a pan of water and held my breath. I figured that I could hold my breath longer than these bugs, and when I ran out of air, the bugs would be dead.

Repeating my new breakfast routine netted the same results. Full of determination, I washed the fruit and submerged it underwater, this time for five minutes. I got the same result. Then I began to wonder: "How many of these bugs had I eaten? Are they alive inside of me?" Not knowing the answers to these questions assured me of one thing: I would never eat another mulberry as long as I lived.

The double tenement house adjacent to Miss Elaine had a pear tree suitable for climbing. Although the ground was often littered with pears, I preferred to navigate through the outer branches of the tree, where I could stuff my pockets with my bounty.

Besides our aging black-heart cherry tree and the felled wild cherry tree, another cherry tree grew just beyond the rise of the Field. Technically, the tree belonged to the Douglas family, but Mr. Douglas would let us pick cherries, provided we left the branches intact. This feat was difficult for us, because the most abundant and ripened cherries were beyond our grasp. One person could jump up and down on a branch and shake cherries off the tree, while others gathered them. If I were alone, I would take a chance at reaching cherries by extending my footwork along the branch to its breaking point.

The last time I climbed this tree, I committed the cardinal sin of easing out too far, thereby cracking the limb under my foot. I had no choice but to break the limb containing a rich bounty of cherries, thus leaving a vulnerable wound in the tree, which managed to recover. Guilt caused me to vow to leave this tree off my list of forbidden fruit, and I never climbed it again.

Oh, Blackwater and Tunnel Vision

Backwater Creek and the train tunnel below our house fused my relationship to nature. Our backyard ended as the woods and thickets sloped over the southeast end of the tunnel. The elevation from the tunnel and the single set of train tracks dropped another forty feet. Briar thickets and steep inclines kept this area sparse of human traffic. Whenever I needed solitude, I followed one of the paths that led me to a ledge over the tunnel. From this vantage point, I could watch slow-moving freight trains rumble through the tunnel. Since the distance between the tunnel ledge and where I could have jumped was short, pouncing on top of the train and getting a free ride would have been easy, if I were daring. I never was.

Two factors weighed heavily in my decision not to make this daring leap. First, regardless of how often I had seen movie actors jump from dramatic heights without injury, I could not bring myself to be so foolhardy. Second, if I were to hitch a ride on a train, where would I go, and how would I get back? Thus, I contented myself with the fantasy of traveling as a hobo, while enjoying the comforts of my surroundings.

When our group of boys got together, we normally took a path below Bill's yard, usually with him leading us, to get to the railroad track. Depending on his lead, we trekked along the tracks, making up games and telling stories until we decided to leave the tracks and return to civilization. Sometimes our journey ended at the James River, other times it ended at Harrison Street, and one time it almost ended with our getting into serious trouble.

As we walked the tracks, the only thing we feared was the sound of the "potato car" that carried the railroad detectives. Whenever we saw them, we hid in the bushes. The distinct moaning of these mini-caboose-like cars alerted us, even though the speed at which they traveled often caught us off guard.

Several decaying wooden railroad signs that lined the tracks offered us target practice for our rock-throwing skills. We pelted the signs into oblivion, not considering that we were performing acts of vandalism; rather, we were speeding up the process of destroying signs that had outlived their usefulness. Before we realized it, a potato car containing two men barreled toward us. The men noticed one of the signs we had stoned and brought the potato car to a screeching halt. We jumped across the tracks when they spotted us, and the chase was on. Bill, being the swiftest, had outdistanced them before they could alight. Rand and I, knowing we were in no position to follow Bill, hid in the underbrush, as we watched the two men on the heels of Junie, chasing him along the network of paths towards Bill's yard and the Field.

After the coast was clear, Rand and I made our way along a path that ended on Harrison Street near the Rucker house, knowing that Junie had been caught.

Water dripping from the sandstone rocks on the northeastern side of the tunnel forms icicles during the winter.

To our delight and surprise, we saw Junie safe from harm. His knowledge of escape routes and his youth had worked to his advantage. The hills we roamed were not for the faint of heart, and evidently the men thought that chasing Junie through the woods was not worth the effort. There was to be another event that would test Junie's skill at evasion; I will mention it in the chapter "Race and Other Relations."

Rand and I would find ourselves in another situation in which we responded as one. One day Junie came to us with the exciting news that Bill had discovered a cave on the side of a cliff near the ridge that ran between Madison and Harrison streets. Bill's plan was to claim this area as a meeting place for a club he envisioned. He had found an old mattress that could be used for overnight stays. I began to imagine living as a cave dweller from some prehistoric time.

Bill's discovery was nothing like my mental picture. The cave, situated on a cliff about thirty feet above the railroad track, made my heart jump when I saw how high and dangerous its location was. We had to climb on a narrow ledge and crawl into a space with barely room enough for the three of us.

Bill said that he would stand on top of the cliff and lower the mattress; he would depend on Rand and me to haul it into the cave. Rand and I surveyed our situation and decided that attempting to grab hold of the

Tracks near the site where we eluded the railroad detectives. To the left is a reservoir on the Daniels Hill side of Blackwater Creek that has since been torn down. The old Rivermont Bridge is in the background, and to the right is one of the cliffs of Garland Hill near Lucado Street.

mattress could lead to somebody falling to his death. We couldn't divulge our fears to Bill, however, because he was our leader. On a count of three, Bill released the mattress, but when it dropped, neither of us attempted to grab it.

We watched as the mattress tumbled onto the tracks below. "I thought you were going to catch the mattress," Bill called down in disgust. "Now look where it's landed...Listen. I hear a train coming. I've got to get that mattress off the track."

Rand and I climbed back to the top of the cliff, where we found no sign of Bill. I was hoping that the oncoming train, which we could not see from our position, would not derail as a result of our ineptitude. We figured that Bill had run down the hill, using his blazing speed, to get to the mattress. Even then we doubted that he reach the mattress before the train arrived.

The western entrance of the tunnel is situated below Hollins Mill Road. We climbed along the path on the left side to get to the street.

Rand and I began our journey through the bushes that led to the end of Harrison Street. To our surprise, we saw Bill ascending one of the paths from the railroad tracks. Shocked at seeing him so soon, we asked where he had been. "Somebody had to move the mattress," he said.

Relieved to know that a train wreck would not be part of my guilty conscience, and puzzled at Bill's rapid return, I asked him how he was able to get the mattress and come back so soon. "I jumped," he said laconically.

We could not believe it. Bill said he had jumped from a distance that to me was a leap of death. But there was no other way to account for his hasty return. We walked home in silence as I played this thirty-foot leap repeatedly in my head. We never visited this cave again, and our dreams of having a secret meeting place remained as distant as the cliffs above.

Pristine water filtered through the cliff rock, causing a perpetual drip near the southeastern end of the tunnel. Someone, we assumed railroad men, had erected a small concrete spring right into the rock, which captured the cool, crystal clear water about a hundred yards before the tunnel's entrance.

Drinking from this spring became part of our journey's ritual. Although the water was clear, it contained sediment that, if agitated, could cloud the water. The sediment hosted crawfish that we could see as we stuck our heads under the covered concrete structure. When we put our hands in the water, trying to capture one of the critters, the crawfish proved to be elusive. If we were lucky enough to pick up one of the creatures before it retreated into the hole in the rock, we would examine our prize and release it back to its domain.

Growing near the spring was a thicket of red raspberries. Timing was the key to eating these berries, which I considered a delicacy of the fruit family. The berries also grew on the path above the Hollins Mill dam, peaking around the first week in August, the time when the woods were least navigable. I often sacrificed bits of skin and blood to get my fill of these soft little berries.

Traveling through the tunnel was not a journey for anyone afraid of the dark. The tunnel curved from the southeastern end to the western end, making it impossible to see from one end to the other. At the crux of the arc, all light ceased to exist for about two seconds. We had to place our hands on the walls as we walked towards daylight to keep from stumbling on the tracks, which were wide enough to accommodate one train and nothing else. Since the tunnel wall was only a few inches from the tracks, we considered any person caught in the tunnel to be doomed.

We ventured through the tunnel only when we were assured a train had just passed through. Once on the other side, we could decide on one of many exploratory options. We could exit from the western end of the tunnel and climb up its right side towards the beginning of Hollins Mill Road. Scaling this side of the tunnel included the benefit of picking huckleberries that grew dangerously close to the edge. The lure of these rare berries was no match for the death we faced, so we didn't often push our luck.

We could go a few yards farther along the tracks and descend to the path along Blackwater Creek, opting to journey to the dam and the antiquated but still functioning Hollins Mill. We could climb through the woods near the opposite end of the tunnel, winding up at the smokestack and dumpsite of Lynchburg General Hospital. Or we could follow the tracks until we reached one of the paths that led to the beginning of Jackson or Polk Street.

About two hundred yards from the western end of the tunnel, the train tracks forked. One branch paralleled the tracks of the high trestle, while the other branch became the low trestle that spanned Blackwater Creek. The high trestle towered some seventy-five feet above the low one. The high trestle I feared, but the low one brought me closer to death.

On one of our journeys, Bill, Paul, Junie, and I followed the tracks crossing the low trestle towards the tunnel. The train tracks upon which we journeyed had been laid after ancient engineers had blasted a swath through one of the area's many hills. Since the tracks curved around a bend, it was impossible to hear or see a train coming if we were crossing the low trestle.

We had no knowledge of train schedules, so crossing the trestle unscathed depended totally on luck. Paul gambled and ran across the trestle.

Looking up from Blackwater Creek at both low and high trestles

70

To show my courage, I went next. My courage waned after a few steps, as Paul stood on the other side, laughing and taunting like a conquering hero.

My hesitancy produced squirrel-like actions. I scampered to the beginning of the trestle, then returned to the tracks, still in doubt about my course of action. Junie helped me make a decision when he called me to come back after I had made another tentative foray on the trestle. Relieved that I could now save face, I trotted back to safety, when, in less than five seconds, a train roared by us.

We stood safely on the side of the tracks as my heart eased its way to my mouth while I thought about what could have been my fate. Had I been on the trestle when the train came, I would have had less than three seconds to jump about forty feet into the shallow part of Blackwater Creek, breaking no less than both of my legs or, worse, ending my life. From that moment on, I have always felt indebted to Junie for saving my life, and the consequences of any mischief that he got me into would pale in comparison to not being able to get into any trouble at all.

The tracks of the high trestle were far more intimidating than the lower ones. The trestle bridged the gap between Tinbridge Hill and Rivermont, spanning a one-hundred-fifty-yard chasm that dropped over one hundred feet to Blackwater Creek. To me the high trestle represented one of the greatest engineering marvels in the city. Stories had been told of men who leaped to their death from the trestle.

We often talked about crossing the high trestle, but fear of oncoming trains discouraged us—that is, until one day, as we were coming from Jefferson Park Pool, a train passed us, heading north across the trestle toward Rivermont.

Bill, Paul, Junie, Rand, and I saw this as the perfect opportunity cross the tracks without fear of an approaching train. Bill, Paul, and Junie took the initiative and started the journey. I was more tentative. "Don't look down," they advised. I inched across the railroad ties until reaching a point where an overwhelming fear gripped me. I stood paralyzed, as insecurity and doubt replaced my juvenile machismo.

The group waited as I attempted to regain my courage. I walked to the same spot, determined to go farther, but once again, I looked down. I could not bring myself to take another step to cross this intimidating distance, even though the railroad ties were wider than the sidewalks in our neighborhood. I watched in defeat as my braver friends made their way to

The high trestle as seen from Hollins Mill Road

the unknown land across the expanse, while I had to content myself with walking under the trestle, examining the massive structure, while assuring myself that I had made the right decision. My only consolation was that Rand also couldn't bring himself to cross the tracks, making both of us miss the experience of a lifetime.

No matter how many times I viewed the trestle, none of my visions led to my crossing it. The trestle represented a limit to what I would attempt to do for the satisfaction of overcoming a fear. It also represented uncertainty and doubt about my abilities.

Blackwater Creek, though polluted, flowed peacefully through the hills of Lynchburg and must have played a major role in carving minor valleys throughout the city's terrain. The creek served as a source of recreation, especially near the place we called Horseshoe Bend, which had a small sandy area we used as a beach and day camp. Since Junie was a good swimmer, he took to the water more readily than I. His proficiency worked against him when, in the summer of 1954, he contracted typhoid fever from the creek. The Health Department quarantined Junie for two weeks, and anyone who had been in recent contact with him had to receive a series of typhoid shots. The health official told our community that one of the shots was guaranteed to make us sick.

Each person had to trek down to the Health and Welfare Department, located on the hillside on Eleventh Street between Clay and Court streets. Most of the people in our neighborhood got sick after the first shot, but not me. I concluded that I had a stronger constitution and was immune to the nausea and other side effects they suffered. I strutted around like a bantam rooster, all sixty-five pounds of me—until the next shot. While everyone else had adjusted to the first shot, my stomach, violated by my food, churned and forced it to spew out of my mouth. As I agonized in intestinal pain and increased my visits to our bathroom, my friends taunted me as I had done them.

By 1955, we had explored much of Blackwater Creek from its mouth at the James River to the rear of the construction site of the new Lynchburg General Hospital. We took advantage of the temporary construction road to travel through the woods unimpeded by briars and thick brush. As we traveled along this newly formed dirt passageway, we picked up scraps of brightly covered copper wire—souvenirs from wiring projects we did not understand. Other than plait the wire, we could find no other use for it.

The journey increased our thirst, which we sought to slake after stumbling upon what appeared to be a clear pool of water. In the tradition of movie stars who found oases in deserts, we cupped our hands, scooped up the water, and quenched our parched throats.

Then we stumbled upon what we assumed to be a discarded metal cement mixer that we thought suitable for floating on the creek. Under Bill's instructions, we pulled the five-by-five-foot vessel to Horseshoe Bend. We were not dressed for water, so we had to postpone our maiden voyage.

We went home unaware that we were in for a night of interminable suffering. The pool of water from which we had drunk, though clear, was also stagnant. Whatever bacteria that swarmed invisibly in our oasis did likewise in our digestive tracts. All of us became violently ill, throwing up to exhaustion. It wasn't until the next day, when we began to compare notes about our illnesses, that we concluded that the water was the source of our maladies.

I then thought about how stupid and desperate we had been to quench our thirst on water not connected to a flowing stream or any other source of fresh water. Our wilderness survival was a lesson that need not have been taught if we had used common sense. Then again, common sense and youthful impetuosity travel divergent paths.

After recovering from our illness, we journeyed back to Horseshoe Bend to try out our new boat. Bill had a pole that would be used to power the boat through the water batteau-style. The boat floated just fine until we got in it. Then buoyancy departed, and the boat slowly began taking on water. We scooped water out with our hands as we made our way back to the sandy shore. Disappointed at the results, after all the hard work it had taken to steal this contraption, we pulled it to the side, abandoning it and our dreams of a Tom and Huck adventure down unassuming Blackwater Creek.

Pool Days

Jefferson Park Pool offered us welcome relief from the heat and boredom associated with summer doldrums. This relief sometimes came at a price.

We had several options in journeying to the pool. If we were lucky, Junie's Uncle George loaded us into his truck, negating the long trek we otherwise faced. We could walk through the streets, about a mile trip, or cut across the dump and save fifteen minutes of travel time. Most of the time we opted for the dump.

Our shortcut could be divided into distinct phases. We first walked the uninterrupted Hollins Street sidewalk for six blocks before the fun began. Once the street ended, we had to walk across the double set of train tracks near the end of the high trestle. Then, opting for one of two pathways, we would run at full speed down the winding gully, like slaloming skiers minus the skis. One misstep and our momentum hurled us into an encounter with unforgiving briars.

We then crossed the single set of train tracks that led to the lower trestle. From there we navigated through a short path lined with underbrush, then crossed the sewage pipe spanning the infamous Shitty Creek, one of two so-named creeks that emptied into Blackwater Creek.

After crossing the pipe, we scaled the steep hill upon which sat the city dump. As we ascended the hill, a stream of wastewater cascaded down along the left side of our path, emptying raw sewage into Shitty Creek below.

If all went well, we could walk across the dump and officially be in Dearington, where, on the hill above, homes bordered this refuse site. If the city was burning refuse, we had to find another way to get to our destination.

We crossed Pulaski Street and walked toward the swings on the Dearington playground. Standing on a hillside looking west, we could see the pool site almost hidden by the willow trees and winding road as we prepared to press forward down the hill.

The direction and speed of our descent to the "promised land" depended on how much pool fever we were experiencing. We could be civil and walk down the path next to the concrete steps designed as seats for softball games. We could walk near the sloping end, where the elevation posed no challenge. Or we could, once again, descend at breakneck speed down the steepest part of the hill and rely on coordination to save us from falling flat on our faces as the hill came to an abrupt end. We always chose the third option, thus making our entry into the pool more enjoyable.

The price of admission was fifteen cents, which didn't always come easily. Sometimes we had to hustle to get the money. Since we were too young to work, we scoured our neighborhood and homes for soft drink bottles that yielded a two-cent deposit. If we were lucky, we would find a Par-T-Pak quart-sized bottle that brought a whopping five-cent bounty. Quart-sized beer bottles yielded five cents, as well, but usually these bottles didn't stray too far from the consumers.

Swimming confirmed my slowness at learning new skills. My mother told me that I didn't start walking or talking until I was two, so when Junie and I took swimming lessons at around age nine, I made limited progress, while he excelled.

My main issue with swimming was an inability to keep my head above water. No matter how hard I tried, every time I tried to lift my head to breathe, the pool water sucked me under. Junie quickly mastered this technique and moved to the advanced group. I languished with the beginners, learning the flutter kick under the instruction of Carl F. Pinn, my future gym teacher.

Mr. Pinn held a graduation ceremony in which he awarded medals for the best students in each phase of instruction. In order to receive an award, students competed for honors. I thought that I could win an award because, had I been able to keep my head above water, I wouldn't be classified as a beginner.

Our first event was the flutter kick, in which I claimed superiority... in my mind. When the chips were down, I discovered there were other boys who had the same idea. At the sound of Mr. Pinn's whistle, we kicked, splashing water everywhere, while holding on to the ledge of the pool. Soon my legs began to falter and my muscles to ache, begging me to stop. I looked to my left, then to my right. Other boys continued kicking. I was determined to endure this ordeal and get a medal. My legs, though, did not share the same sentiment. The elasticity went out of them, forcing me to relinquish my quest for fame.

Disappointed, I had one other opportunity to medal. Our final category, holding one's breath underwater, was mine for the taking. The contest wasn't even close. Neither was I. I held my breath until I felt like I was getting "the bends." When I finally gasped for air with the anticipation of victory, one final student remained. I watched as my hope for a medal stayed submerged with the head of Thomas White, a much older yet less competent swimmer than I. Not only did he hold his breath longer, he did it by about forty-five seconds. I would have drowned had I been under water that long. This added insult to injury: being defeated by a non-swimmer.

Junie, on the other hand, won at least three awards, including one for a stroke called the Shall-On pull. I'm sure this is misspelled and mispronounced. It was similar to the sidestroke and involved swimming around the pool's perimeter. One student in his group had swum the stroke, outdistancing all others by a wide margin. When Junie's time came, he not only surpassed his nearest rival but also continued to swim the stroke so effortlessly that he almost lapped the distance of his competition. Mr. Pinn actually had to coax Junie to stop swimming in order for us to begin the award ceremonies.

I received a certificate of completion, like everybody else, but nothing indicating that I was extraordinary. Junie said he thought I would at least get a medal for holding my breath. I was happy for him but also wished I had something to salve my now sorely bruised ego.

For years I swam with my head down. My early success in swimming came only when I swam on my bed, dreaming that I could use this dry technique when I encountered water. Each time, though, I failed. My breakthrough came when I was thirteen, at summer camp, where my swimming instructor uttered three simple words that forever changed my relationship to water: "Arch your back."

Instantly and automatically, I could swim and breathe. No more swimming under water, stopping to dog paddle, and tiring myself out. I had a new world in which to swim, but by this time the halcyon days at Jefferson Park were reaching an end.

A day at the pool tested our resolve against blistering sun and formidable terrain. Usually ashened from pool water and the baking rays of the sun, we dragged our weary bodies up winding Hunt Street across the barren baseball field in the park. Weakened, we usually opted to climb the coliseum-like concrete steps, rather than scale the steep hill to the side. Sometimes we walked up the hill with our backs turned, determined to find the most ergonomically satisfying way to conserve energy from our weakened bodies.

Dearington added several dramatic scenes to my life, two of which I escaped with injuries that continue to give me chills when I revert to a classic counterfactual thinking phrase: "What if…?" These two incidents I will recount later.

One of the benefits of crossing the dump on the way to Dearington was scavenging for old car and truck tires. Routinely, items were burned in piles, but if we timed it right, we could salvage tires to play with. If the tires failed to meet our standard for toys, then we would roll them over the hill to see which ones could perform the highest and most acrobatic bounces. If we were impish enough, we would roll the tires near the path as unsuspecting boys descended it. We never hit anyone, and the many ledges on the hillside provided protection as the tires tumbled toward Shitty Creek.

Junie, forever the aggressor, decided that the clods of red dirt near the pool construction site would make suitable missiles for hitting the willow trees that draped the picnic area. After splattering a few clumps near and around the trees, Junie saw a much more exciting target: two boys about our age on the hill above. Junie started lobbing dirt balls, and I reluctantly followed suit.

Being at the bottom of the hill put us at a disadvantage, as the other boys, who seemed to have an unending supply of ammunition, bombarded the trees behind which we were hiding.

When our ammo ran out, Junie was able to flee, while I got trapped. One of the dirt balls thrown by the lefty I knew was James "Gator" Jones hit me on the shoulder. Soon their supply of ammunition dwindled, and I scampered like a frightened rabbit out of harm's way.

It was my misfortune to attend the same church as Gator, Fifth Street Baptist. The following Sunday, Gator, who had a reputation for being tough, saw me as he talked about the incident to some other boys, saying, "That's one of them right there."

I felt like Peter spotted by the Romans after the arrest of Jesus. Fear enveloped my face as I thought of the fine mess Junie had gotten me into once again. Gator grabbed the front collar of my shirt, raising it to my chin and saying, "I ought to whip your ass." I remained silent, not wanting to antagonize him and get the beating I deserved. I think he saw that I was no match for him and granted me clemency because I had on my Sunday clothes. I skulked away, until I got far enough to run without being seen.

Although crossing the dump sounds distasteful, it often provided us with excitement and experiences we could not find elsewhere.

One of my aunts lived in Dearington on Chambers Street, which bordered the dump. She had an apple tree in the backyard of her little bungalow that bore small but delicious fruit. Since I had visited her only once or twice, she couldn't distinguish me from other youth who sought to pick from her tree.

Regardless, I was confident that I stood in her good graces and led our group to her house to ask for apples. Her response was a cackling "No." Dejected, we decided to take matters into our own hands; we eased alongside the bushes that partially hid the tree and began picking apples. Suddenly we heard "Get outta my tree," accompanied by the sound of a gunshot that we swore rustled the branches of the trees above us. We hauled our butts across the dump until we felt we were out of range.

"I thought she was some kin to you," Bill said. "She is," I said, trying to catch my breath, "but that don't make her nice."

One journey down the dump temporarily destroyed my confidence and embarrassed me to no end. We had descended to the bottom of the hill of the dump ready to make our way across Shitty Creek when I lost my balance and slipped in. The creek was only about two feet deep, but the humiliation that accompanied the fall caused me to shed tears of shame. Bill pulled me out and tried to comfort me, but I could hear the snickering over my sobs as I looked at the soaked blue shorts that Momma had made.

I could now claim to be one of two people who fell in the creek. William Green had done it before, but I felt I was more coordinated than he was and should have been on a different skill level. My soiled pants, however, told another story.

In the summer of 1955, my first serious injury, compliments of the dump, originated from a pair of shoes that I had worn to the pool. The sole of my right shoe had separated from the top, causing it to flap like a clown's shoe. Wearing socks was a waste of time because dirt and gravel would have worn them out.

From the top of the hill of the dump, we began our rapid descent, at full speed, as usual. I was side-by-side with Junie, determined to pass him at the first opportunity, when I veered off the path slightly. Then I felt it. The sharpest pain I had ever experienced sent chills up and down my spine as I looked at my exposed right big toe sliced deeply from a piece of tin that stuck out from the path.

Before I even looked down, a worst-case scenario flashed through my brain: "I've cut my toe off." Fortunately, the cut was deep, but the tip of the toe held fast. No tears flowed this time, just anger at having on that crappy pair of shoes.

Somehow I made it home, and Momma dressed the wound before taking me to the emergency room of the relocated Lynchburg General Hospital. This was the first time I had been to the new hospital since our group of boys had followed Blackwater Creek to its construction site.

The toe had stopped bleeding, but the throbbing pain continued. We waited for about two hours before someone attended to me. Unlike the compassionate white doctor who took care of me after my sledding accident, this doctor seemed indifferent to my injury and recommended that I get stitches. I don't know the details of his conversation with Momma, but she detected racism and decided to seek medical assistance from a black general practitioner, Dr. Eldorado Johnson, who, along with her brother, Walter, had built an office and adjoining Teenage Canteen at the corner of Fifth and Polk streets.

After looking at my wound, Dr. Johnson decided stitches would make healing worse and leave a bigger scar. She patched me up as Momma looked on. Momma had to go back to work, so she left me bus fare to get back home.

I hobbled across the street and stood at the bus stop. I waited patiently, trying to figure out how to get on the bus without exacerbating the pain. As the bus approached, I felt relieved that I would soon be home. The white bus driver, though, must have assumed that a ten-year-old black boy on this corner was waiting to cross the street; he passed me by.

Hopping on my good foot and limping on the heel of my bad one, which was visibly bandaged, I waved him down before he managed to get out of sight. Slowly I limped to the bus, grabbing both step rails as I deposited coins. He apologized for his action, but all I could think about was how his passing me fit into the same behavior that had caused Momma to leave the hospital.

The following year led to my most disastrous Dearington-related experience. This time the incident had nothing to do with swimming.

Dearington hosted softball games that attracted black spectators from all over the city and surrounding counties. Mr. Martin, my sixth-grade teacher, had the responsibility of turning out the lights whenever the games were over. If his schedule permitted, he would give rides on a first-come, first-served basis to anyone who would get to his Hudson Hornet.

On this particular night, Junie and I were standing on top of the plateau that overlooked the baseball diamond. When the game ended, we geared up for our downhill flight at breakneck speed. I felt I had the advantage of being in the inside lane and would claim the honor of being the first one to reach our teacher.

Then it happened. Dutifully, Mr. Martin turned off the lights. We were in mid-flight. I took another step, but my foot failed to hit the ground. In a nanosecond I realized that my course had veered over the steps, and before I could brace myself, I fell face first on the top concrete step. Stars shot out of my head, which absorbed most of the initial blow. I tumbled down each of the nine steps, picking up an assortment of wounds on the way.

My screams resonated from the bottom step, as Mr. Martin, who had heard my first thud and ensuing whimpering, approached me with a flashlight in his hand. Instantly my forehead had swollen to a cartoonish egg-sized lump as Junie and others gathered around, looking on more in amusement than in awe.

Mr. Martin escorted me up the hill near Kirby Street, opposite where I had fallen, and bathed my head in the cold water of the nearby drinking fountain. Though he was helpful and sympathetic, he had to restrain himself from chuckling at the size of my knot, which was not my only injury. As he soothed my head, I felt the stinging from a split right above the middle of my top lip, while my arms and legs ached from my newly acquired scrapes.

Mr. Martin gave us a lift to Fifth and Federal streets, where our destinations diverged. When I arrived home, I slinked my way upstairs to examine my wounds. Though in pain, I had to chuckle at the size of my knot, which had shrunk somewhat. My lip wound wasn't as severe as the stinging suggested, but I discovered another wound that I had overlooked. Feeling a throbbing in my side, I lifted my shirt and saw a gaping hole in my side, just above my right hip.

After evaluating my injuries, I took the advice of Mr. Martin and applied ice to my head, hoping it would shrink further before I went to school the next day. By the time I got to Mr. Martin's class, I had traces of the knot, but it was not large enough to elicit sixth-grade teasing.

I still get squeamish when I think that I could have lost the tip of my toe at the dumpsite or split my head open on the steps. As I look back on these two incidents, I am grateful that my childhood injuries were relatively minor.

One of the pitfalls of our journeys to the pool was finding it closed. This gut-wrenching discovery came once we got to the top of the hill near the steps, where we saw no signs of life. The pool needed regular cleaning, and since our channels of communication left much to be desired, we were often out of the loop regarding pool closings.

Another disappointment we faced at the pool came from the acrobatics of Moonie Mullins. Two of the most skillful divers to spring off the Jefferson Park diving board were Moonie Mullins and Jimmy Brown. Jimmy, whose smile was as impressive as his diving, could complete a one-and-a-half somersault in Olympic form, entering the water with barely a ripple. Moonie, on the other hand, having springs in his powerful legs, sought to elevate to the clouds when he hit the board. To increase his height, Moonie would climb onto one of the pilings above and beside the diving board, and, with cat-like coordination, pounce on the board to achieve extra recoil from his massive legs. This was a stunt he did about once a year, because when he hit the board, everyone in the pool would hear a resounding crack, as the wooden plank yielded to the added stress.

Once the board was cracked, it was seldom repaired until the next season. We all hoped that we could get a few dives in before Moonie made his appearance. Most of the time, we had to be content just diving in the ten-foot section.

Jefferson Park Pool would close permanently when a group of black activists sought to integrate Miller Park Pool. The city, as stubborn as any other racist entity, closed all city-managed pools rather than allow blacks and whites an opportunity to enjoy each other's company.

Within a week, dump trucks convoyed to the pool and filled it with loads of dirt. The willow trees were cut down, and within the blink of an eye, every vestige of our pool and its landmarks was buried and landscaped. Miller Park would reopen, but for us, a part of our culture had been destroyed. Such destruction and distortion proved to be a consistent strategy used against African Americans of my generation.

Hot Wheels

Movement is the opiate of youth, and the hills of our community graced us with an ideal environment where we could move at daring speeds. Besides the disastrous trial run on my bicycle, I, like every other youth in Tinbridge Hill, owned a pair of roller skates.

For my sixth Christmas I told Momma I wanted my first pair of skates. Some of my friends had vintage Union skates that clamped onto the soles of shoes. I anticipated Santa Claus bringing me a pair. On Christmas Day Santa came through, but he must have gotten me mixed up with a younger kid, for when I went downstairs to get my highly anticipated Union skates, I saw a pair of red and yellow plastic strap-ons.

Using these skates was only one short step above walking. I felt degraded because all my peers had the standard iron-wheel, fast-rolling Unions, while my skates only rolled when I pumped them. I could not even drift down the sidewalk. I expressed my disappointment to Momma, but either she lacked knowledge of my skills or didn't have the money to upgrade to metal.

The next year, though, I got my first pair of Union skates, and from then on I joined the ranks of skaters who challenged every hill and tried every imaginable trick. Since our McKinley Street sidewalk extended only two house-lengths, skating on it quickly became dull. The only challenge was to skate backwards, take flight when the sidewalk ended, and land on the asphalt in front of our house.

Skating on the sidewalk in front of the Douglas house was safe, which is why we opted for the street instead. We skated down Federal Street, jumping on the sidewalk should a car should appear. Here we perfected our skills as we practiced moves such as the painful "Eagle split."

Our repertoire also included the squat, where we lowered ourselves as close to the ground as possible and clasped our arms together; the squat thrust, which was the same move with one leg extended, essentially skating on six wheels; the flying cross, where we skated on one foot and leaned forward, extending our limbs parallel to the ground; the backwards flying cross; tip-toe skating, using the front wheels only; and the same move backwards, by far our wobbliest maneuver.

As we became more proficient, we took on the city, skating throughout the uncharted neighborhoods of College Hill, Rivermont, White Rock Hill, and Chestnut Hill.

Our most challenging skating took place on Polk Street. Starting from the top of the hill at Garland, where I used to live, the elevation dropped sixty-five feet in two blocks. We would speed down the hill until tears streamed from our eyes. In most cases, we picked up enough speed in the first block to satisfy our thrill-seeking obsession. At this juncture, I would veer onto the grass in front of the Evans house, while Junie, always more daring, would push on.

Eventually I got up enough nerve to complete the two-block journey. By then Junie had begun to come down Polk Street backwards. I had to keep up, so I also came down the hill backwards, using tiptoeing. This approach to fanciness was short-lived because the extreme wobble and the fear of falling sapped my nerve. It appeared that Junie had once again bested me.

The blocks between Second and Fourth streets were more daunting. This hill was more suitable for sleds and bicycles than skates. But excitement called. Skating from Third Street to Second was thrilling enough; however, skating from Fourth Street meant not being able to see the bottom of the hill for a whole block. My most daring ride came when I skated from Fourth to Second without having my skates clamped to my saddle oxfords. This was one time my foolishness did not end in disaster.

Union skates, although the most popular brand, had a competitor, Rollfast, that was cheaper with a newer style clamp. I bought a pair of these bargain skates from S.O. Fisher's Sporting Goods Store on Main Street and on my inaugural run took them for a spin to my Aunt Pearl's house on Second Street, midway between Monroe and Polk.

The intersection at Polk and Second represented the nadir of our community. From this point both streets went uphill, which meant I had to go downhill before I could get to Aunt Pearl's. I opted to go down Second Street from Jackson, behind Yoder School.

Getting into my famous crouch, I pumped my body up and down to generate extra speed. Without warning, the front axle of my right skate split, sending the two wheels careening into the bushes and putting me into an instant limp as I fought to keep my balance. I escaped the embarrassment of falling as I lamely approached Lewis Diggs's house to my right and the Steeples' house on the left. But I vowed that never again would I buy a pair of Rollfast skates.

Riding my bike demonstrated without a doubt that my brain had not ripened. Junie, Bill, Paul, and Mitchell invited me to take my maiden voyage down Hollins Mill Road. I followed them hesitatingly because I was unfamiliar with the turns or the speed. As a result, I liberally applied the brakes, while losing ground and my dignity for being so far behind. I tried to explain my timidity to no avail; I was the bicycle chicken.

To overcome my fear and to prove my bravado, I decided to redeem myself by retaking this journey alone. I would show my friends I had a backbone. The next day I set out to prove to myself, at least, that I could negotiate this treacherous street. I had one slight problem: the chain on my bike had broken.

Undaunted, I walked my bike down McKinley Street to Hollins Mill Road and jumped on. I knew that no chain meant no brakes. My friends hadn't used brakes when they rode down the hill; having no chain would guarantee that I wouldn't either.

I swung my leg over the frame and threw caution to the wind. My bike picked up momentum, finally going faster than I had ever been on a bike in my life. Curves jumped out at me, my fear increasing proportionately with my speed. Panic replaced fear as I tried to figure out how to stop this runaway bike. I was rapidly approaching a clearing about thirty feet below the McCoy house and knew that this was my point of no return.

I turned my bike toward the hillside, hoping the embankment would buffer my speed and stop me. I envisioned this scene without carefully surveying the landscape, which included a rotten log in my path. My bicycle hit the log and tossed me like I was an inexperienced bronco rider.

I landed safely in the bushes, dazed but not bruised. My bicycle was not so lucky. After I shook the cobwebs out of my empty head, I retrieved my bike to begin the long trek home. The handlebars and the fork of the front wheel were bent, causing me to have to point the handlebars in one direction in order to guide the bike in another.

As I walked up the hill contemplating my failed attempt to make history, my thoughts turned to my stupidity. What was I thinking about? This was one of the dumbest things I had ever done. Even so, when I got back on the hill, I told Junie and Bill what had happened. They looked at me with blank expressions, which I read to mean the same thing I had already admitted to myself: that this was one of the most insane things I could have done.

More sensibly, I raced Junie down Federal Street, starting at Second, confident that my bike, now refurbished, possessed the speed needed to win our contest. Junie soon began to pull ahead, as I pumped furiously, getting no appreciable acceleration in speed. He looked back as the gap between us widened. I was soundly defeated.

When we got off our bikes, I noticed that my back wheel lacked sufficient air and had been rubbing against the frame. I showed Junie why I couldn't keep up and challenged him to a rematch. Junie had a hard-and-fast rule in playing: no second chances. I would see him enforce this rule in other sports that we played. I, on the other hand, didn't mind giving a person another chance, but I understood if I couldn't beat Junie in my first attempt, I would never get another.

A bicycle race I had with Mitchell had more physically lasting consequences. Our route was to race down McIvor Street, turn around at the spur road across from the dewberry patch, and make the return trip to Junie's house. Mitchell had about a half-length lead on me as we made the turn-off. I saw my opportunity to get in front of him by cutting to the inside. Mitchell held his ground, forcing me to the outside. My devious mind figured that if I tapped his back wheel, then he would lose his balance and I would avenge all my lost challenges to him.

My blind ambition, though, had failed to take into account that back wheels are more stable than front ones. When our tires met, my balance was the one that went awry. I slid in the dirt, while Mitchell kept going, slowing down after hearing the sound of metal, flesh, and gravel collide.

I got up mad, accusing him of deliberately sabotaging the race. Mitchell reminded me, "You cut in front of me." It didn't matter to me. He should have let me cut in front. I brushed myself off and peeled down my pants, exposing my left hip, where a quarter-sized "strawberry" adorned my skin.

I was mad at Mitchell, but even madder at myself, for I knew had I been in the lead, I would have made the same move that Mitchell had made. Now, I have a permanent scar to remind me of my foolish attempt at victory. More important, it serves as a reminder of how I, like many people, seek to blame others for my own mistakes.

One other means of neighborhood transportation brought together resourcefulness and creativity: the hotrod. We depended on the aftermath of Soap Box Derby contests to supply us with the basic need of our hotrods, the wheels. Paul had access to two-by-six-inch boards we used for the hotrod chassis, thanks to Pappy DeLoatch. We scoured yards, alleys, and fields looking for discarded tricycles and wagons that we could cannibalize for axles and other hotrod parts.

Once we assembled our Flintstone-era vehicles, we field-tested them on the slope of McIvor Street. One of my most painful rides occurred when Paul invited me to ride with him to the end of the cul-de-sac on the maiden voyage of his latest hotrod model. By far my most gregarious friend, Paul chuckled as he convinced me to stand on the frame and hold onto his shoulders as he negotiated his way down the hill.

We quickly picked up speed, causing me to realize the disadvantage of my position. I urged Paul to slow down, but he blurted out a Vincent Price laugh as we approached the cul-de-sac. He swerved around the curve with tires moaning as inertia and centripetal force took the hotrod in one direction, while centrifugal force took me in another.

Paul had the advantages of holding fast to the rope that steered the wheels and having a lower center of gravity. I, on the other hand, was at the mercy of the strength of my grip, which was extremely tenuous. As he skidded to a halt, I didn't. Loosening my grip, I obeyed Newton's first law of motion and continued along the orbit to which I had been assigned. When I finally hit the ground, I tumbled onto the asphalt as Paul chortled like Santa Claus.

I got up wincing in pain, noticing how much of my seersucker shirt and skin had been sacrificed to the asphalt gods. My minor abrasion stung enough just to be irritating, but I considered Paul my main irritant at that moment, because he had no compassion for my injury.

Paul and I journeyed back to McKinley Street, where I sought the comfort and aid of Momma. She dressed my wound in a way that I would never forget. Our standard first-aid treatments included gentian violet and Mercurochrome. Since Momma worked at the hospital, she had access to other medical supplies, including something called Merthiolate. Her description of the power of this flame-colored liquid had me anticipating instant healing. As soon as she applied it to my raw skin, pain shot through my body as I snatched away. Momma quizzically looked at me as my eyes watered.

"What's wrong?" she asked. "It hurts!" was my simple reply. Looking at me as though I was "puttin' on," she said, "It couldn't hurt that much. I just put a little on you." "Yeah, but that little bit hurt," I said. Disregarding my theatrics and thinking the worst was over, she applied another dab, and I repeated my performance. Then she concluded that maybe the pain I felt was real. This marked my first and last encounter with Merthiolate. Considering the number of high-risk antics I experienced, I was fortunate to survive with only scrapes and bruises.

Fun and Games

Playing marbles became part of my socialization once I honed my skills. I discovered mastery over my peers when I first played for keeps in the second grade. My shooting technique of aim, squeeze, and shoot gave me an advantage over children who used their thumbs to flip or hunch their "shooting toy."

I entered my first shooting match in the Yoder School sandbox, anteing up five marbles like other second- and third-graders. When my turn came, I knocked out one marble, stuck in the ring, and proceeded to have my way with my opponents' marbles.

Boys young and old stood around, watching in amazement as I "cleaned up," until Albert Eubanks, one of the older ones, decided to expand the ring. My shooting style did not favor large rings, because I could only squeeze marbles so hard. Before my weakness was exposed, the bell rang. For the next few years, each spring I would take a few marbles to school and arrive home with a pocketful.

A house at the corner of Second and Federal streets displayed in its window a gallon glass jar filled with marbles. I would admire that jar every time I passed the house and wondered how long it would take for me to acquire such a collection.

My marble collection eventually filled this gallon jar.

The other downside to my shooting style was the undue pressure it put on my thumbnail. By the fourth grade, I noticed that my

91

fingernail was beginning to crack. At first I didn't pay any attention to it, but soon it began to affect my aim, interfering with my winning ways and goal of accumulating a gallon jar of marbles.

My thumbnail, an integral part of my marble dominance, was molting like a cicada. I could not hit a marble one inch in front of me. The pain would make squeezing marbles unbearable. As the marble season waned, a new thumbnail replaced the old one. The next year I experienced the same phenomenon.

I knew that if I were to reach my goal of a gallon of marbles, I would have to change my style, which I did. I learned how to re-shoot, practicing in the dirt of my front yard in the summer and on the wooden floor at the base of our front room steps in the winter. By the time I left the seventh grade, I had garnered hundreds of marbles, a collection that I still maintain today. Many of these marbles came from my Harrison Street friends Steve and the late George "Champ" Rucker, who liked to reminisce about how I hustled them.

A measure of our resourcefulness was our ability to use the environment to compensate for a lack of commercial toys. Fall was the best time to play cowboys and Indians because the ubiquitous ailanthus, commonly referred to as the tree of heaven but known to us as the stinkwood tree, shed its trifoliate leaves to provide arrows for our bows. We harvested leaf stems, examined their potential as arrow shafts, and bent bottle caps over the tips for arrowheads. For more dangerous arrowheads we substituted metal points crafted out of coat hangers. We avoided shooting at each other, but Miss Elaine's bantam chickens were fair game.

The thrill of the hunt usually resulted in a lot of near misses as we chased the elusive chickens through the thickets separating Miss Elaine's yard from the Field. I got lucky one time when one of my non-tipped arrows landed in a chicken's butt. I don't know if it penetrated the skin or got stuck in the feathers; as far as I was concerned, I was a bona fide hunter.

We searched the woods for wood good for bows. The stinkwood tree was too porous and inflexible to make suitable bows. Cedar limbs made the most flexible bows, but these trees were scarce. When we got our bows and arrows finished, the next step would be to find a suitable steed. For this we returned to the ubiquitous stinkwood.

To make our horses, we sought out the sturdiest stinkwood sapling, which we felled by axe or, more commonly, by brute force. We had the option of maintaining the skin on the bark, shaving it to simulate pinto ponies, or skinning it to its milky white dermis, thereby giving the color of most cowboy heroes' horses.

Relying on our imaginations and the memories of our favorite western heroes, from Hopalong Cassidy to the Lone Ranger, we galloped through the Field, cap guns blazing. As a demonstration of mastery and control over our stick horses, we would plant the base on the ground, similar to a pole-vaulter. For a brief moment we defied gravity as our feet lifted in the air, trying our best to emulate the horse-rearing techniques of our heroes.

Eventually our sticks would break from the strain of countless repetitions of horse-rearing. If the trauma occurred close enough to the base of the stick, we could amputate it and use the rest as a pony. Most of the time, a crack sounded the death knell of our faithful steed, and we either ended our play or sought another stick from our endless corral.

The magnetic pull of the Field brought together friends from all parts of our small community. We cut our teeth on playing softball and touch football when the Field was unplowed.

In order to take advantage of the main part of the Field and the sloping side that ended in the thicket just beyond where McKinley Street should have been, we had to establish ground rules for softball. Balls could be hit anywhere in the Field, but if they landed in the bushes on the fly, it was an automatic out. Consequently, we hit a lot of ground balls to ensure we could get on base.

Power hitters like Gaulie Wright sometimes threw caution to the wind and hit for distance. When he or some of the others got up to bat, the outfielders were stationed at the bottom of the Field. Strategically, the outfielders would be unable to see the batter and relied on the second baseman to announce the direction of any fly ball beyond his reach. It was up to the outfield to anticipate where the ball would head and then try to make a play on it. This type of baseball-playing improved our abilities to estimate how far a ball would travel by the sound it made on the bat and developed our reflexes to respond to unexpected bounces should the ball hit the ground.

My first exposure to softball came through my brother Lafayette, who let me use one of his gloves when I was seven years old. Since I was right-handed, putting a glove on my left hand to catch a ball was a foreign experience. When he tossed me my first ball, I awkwardly twisted my glove in front of me and caught the ball with my face.

After recovering from the minor blood that oozed from my lip, I asked him for the first-baseman's mitt, which I put on my right hand. I deemed my left hand useless as I caught with the glove on my right hand and took it off to throw. Forever the slow learner, I had a difficult time adjusting to wearing a baseball glove appropriately.

To compensate for my ineptitude, I would pretend to be the Brooklyn Dodger left-handed pitcher, Sal Maglie, as I continued to catch with the glove on my right hand, while feebly throwing with my left. Other times I would toss the ball straight up with my right hand and quickly put the glove back on the same hand in time to catch it. Slowly, I discovered that the fallacy of my catching would limit my ability to play with anyone other than myself. Eventually my coordination developed well enough for me to use the glove properly.

Learning how to hold and swing a bat posed easily correctable problems. Once I learned how to hold the bat the right way, I swung like a natural lefty. I think this originated from holding a broom and sweeping from left to right. Since most of the guys hit right-handed, I learned how to hit from that side of the plate. Tucker would tell me, "Oh, you want to be a switch-hitter like Mickey Mantle." I took this as a compliment.

Once I got older, I saved up enough to buy my first glove, a Wilson outfield glove autographed by Don Zimmer. Soon I was coordinated enough to become a fair softball player on our small playing field. This training would serve me well when I got an opportunity to play Little League baseball for the Tinbridge Hill team.

My Polk Street friends, under the initial encouragement of Percy Coles, Sr., who lived in the first house on Jackson Street, formed a ragtag neighborhood team, devoid of any resources. This group included James "Boodie" Anderson, Roger and Linwood Coles, James and Silas Herndon, Wheeler "Wee Wee" Hughes, James Norfleet, Clarence Patrick, Bobby Reid Cook, Sterling "Dog" Traynham, and Granville Burnette.

We practiced in the small lot next to Mr. Percy's house, but this limited our ability to learn some of baseball's nuances. Because Mr. Percy had never seen me play, he assigned me to left field. Soon, after watching me field balls missed by our shortstop, he placed me in that position.

By the time I began playing baseball, my Wilson glove had seen its best days. All the padding had migrated to the heel of my glove, exposing my hand to a stinging pain if I caught balls in the wrong spot. Mr. Percy and the rest of the team referred to my glove as tissue paper, since it had no padding, but it served me well during the initial year that I transitioned from softball to hardball.

In our first game, played on the field below Dunbar High School, we faced a veteran and uniformed White Rock Hill team. Our team, green from no real practicing and without a consistent coach, showed our mettle, trailing by one run in the last inning. We had runners on second and third with two outs when I came up to bat.

I approached home plate and stepped deep in the batter's box, using the stance I had learned from reading the hitting instructions of Nellie Fox, a former Chicago White Sox player. Chili Quarles, the catcher, issued a mild protest that I was too close to him, but I knew the rules, and the umpire said, "Play ball."

I was facing Marvin Smith, the diminutive pitcher known for hitting a batter while throwing his curve ball. All of my teammates cheered me on as I took my practice swings. I watched the first pitch whiz by me for ball one. On the second pitch, I fouled. Then, on the third pitch, I heard the unmistakable sound of wood hitting leather and watched the ball I had hit sail toward the gap between the shortstop and left field.

With teammates cheering, I ran towards first base, watching Preston Coleman extend his long arm skyward while jumping in the air. I watched as my moment of heroism faded with cheers now muffled, as his glove engulfed the ball, ending the game.

Our disappointment didn't last, because we had put up a valiant fight. We went home pleased at our showing and full of counterfactual thinking: "If he hadn't caught the ball...."

Over the few years we stayed together, the responsibility of learning the game fell on each player and not on Mr. Percy, who had become our phantom coach. One player who did assume the unofficial role of coach was Linwood Coles, whom we called "Peanut." That nickname would change in dramatic fashion when we practiced in the field next to his house. Peanut, one of the younger members of the team, tried to tell us "veterans" how to play. Soon we began teasing Peanut about his coaching strategies. "You must think you're Casey Stengel, don't you?" somebody said. From then on, every time Peanut would give advice, we would taunt him, saying, "Okay, Casey," or "Anything else, Casey?"

Peanut got irritated and warned us against calling him "Casey." But the taunts continued—until Peanut lost it. Unknown to anyone except his brothers, Roger ("Bones") and Percy, Jr. ("Butch"), Peanut had a violent temper. With tears streaming down his face, he went to the embankment just below

95

Miss Lucy's yard, picked up anything he could hold, and began to sling. An assortment of missiles—planks, bricks, and rocks—whizzed across the field, as he violently chastised us for giving him his new sobriquet.

Realizing that this was not a time for negotiation, we scampered for cover, hiding behind trees and hillsides until Peanut's temper subsided. Slowly we returned to the field, and Peanut, after some thought, decided that Casey was not such a bad name after all. Without fear of retribution, we continued to call him that forevermore.

I wanted to become the most versatile player on our team. I believed that my catching skills were proficient at any field position. The only two positions I had not explored were pitching and hind catching. I had played both positions in softball, but this was different. In one of our practice sessions, I volunteered to be the catcher. Be reminded that we lacked resources, including any type of hind catching equipment, but I felt confident that my skills would compensate for the difference.

The first person to come to bat was Junie, who had remained an outsider to our fledgling team. I squatted down and pounded the inside of the mitt, giving the pitcher, Bones, a suitable target. He delivered the pitch. Junie swung, and I immediately broke the cardinal rule of hind catching: don't blink. The ball tipped the bat and elevated about an inch above the tip of my glove.

When I opened my eyes, the ball was zeroing in on my forehead. Before I had a chance to react, I heard the sound of rawhide hitting bone and saw stars reminiscent of those produced in Dearington. I hit the ground, holding my head. The guys came over, but this time there was no goose egg. I shook it off and got back behind the plate, but I was not the same. The next time I tried to catch, I turned my head and body when Junie swung, causing me to get hit in the back. My ego was not worth the pain. The message was clear: stay in the field and leave hind catching to James "Otis" Norfleet.

To improve my catching coordination and timing, I relied on old golf balls and the Wall on Federal Street. I would stand across the street and throw the golf balls against the Wall, timing myself to ensure I could catch the caroms before cars approached. The harder I threw, the faster the balls returned. Sometimes the balls punished me if I failed to catch them. I would get hit either when I didn't position my glove right or when a missed ball returned from the curb of the sidewalk behind me, hitting me in the back or head. I don't know how much I actually improved, but I did lose a lot of golf balls in the hedges bordering the sidewalk.

My exposure to golf began from my brothers and the older boys on McKinley Street who caddied at the all-white Boonsboro Country Club. The first time I held a golf club in my hand, I added to my list of inaugural disasters. The guys had purchased used clubs from the caddy shack and collected some old golf balls they had found in the woods on the course. They went to the dead-end of McKinley Street and knocked some of the balls over the hill into the woods. When they gave me an opportunity, I went into my left-hand swing using a right-handed club. Trying to hit a golf ball was taxing enough; trying to hit it with the back of the club face was a sad start to learning how to play golf.

When I turned thirteen, I made my first trip to Boonsboro Country Club, about eight miles away. Hitchhiking was the standard mode of transportation for most of us. Usually, Junie, Rand and I went as a group that sometimes included a few other boys from the other side of Tinbridge Hill.

We met at the Wall in front of the Douglas home, or we started our journey at the entrance to Hollins Mill Road. Beginning here became a disadvantage if other boys decided to hitchhike from the block before us. Our hitchhiking started around seven a.m., and we always hoped to catch a ride "all the way" with golfers. Sometime golfers we recognized would knowingly pass right by us, only to use us as caddies after we caught a ride with someone else.

Clarence "Buddy" Crews, my sister's classmate, owned a car and would sometimes give us a ride if he planned to caddy. Other times he would torment us by picking us up at the Wall and dropping us off at the next block, saying, "This is far as I'm going. I hope this helped you out." He would let us out, then make a u-turn at the beginning of McIvor Street, while we took our dejected butts back up the street to start over.

One person guaranteed us a direct trip to the club, but on one occasion it would transform into the ride of our lives. Boodie told me that he and Bones had gotten a ride with this young black guy from Bedford County who said he was a stock car driver. The description of their speeding around the curves of Boonsboro Road sounded like a thrill ride at the fair in Madison Heights. He told them that he came through Hollins Mill Road around seven-thirty, and if we were on the corner, he would pick us up. The three of us highly anticipated his return. When he arrived, I called shotgun and jumped in the front seat. Then the fun began.

True to form, he sped down Hollins Mill Road and turned on Bedford Avenue to Rivermont Avenue, giving us a taste of the ride to come. Salivating at the opportunity to ride faster than I ever had before, I felt my anticipation build as Rivermont Avenue changed to Boonsboro Road. From here on, there were no traffic lights.

With a quick shift of gears, my head snapped back, unable to respond immediately to the change in motion. Then the speed picked up as tires started screeching. We went over one hill doing about seventy-five miles an hour. The car left the ground, and when it came down, I found myself flying toward the dashboard. I quickly extended my hand to keep from going through the windshield. Suddenly I realized that I was riding with a fool.

We rounded the next curve, and we all slid to the right. We could feel the car list to the right as the left tires lost contact with the asphalt. This was definitely not how I envisioned the thrill ride. My heart pounded as we sped along with the driver oblivious to our frightened faces.

We braced ourselves as he made quick work of this eight-mile ordeal. When he dropped us off at the entrance to the club, we gratefully thanked him and vowed to each other never to ride with him again.

Caddying, a natural transition to playing golf, offered us a look at another of our subcultures. A social structure existed in this world that exposed naïve boys like me to hustlers and professional caddies, who enlivened the back of the caddy shack with tales and epic poems. Many of the caddies had completed one of their rites of passage—going to prison—and filled us in on the latest version of the Signifying Monkey, Dolomite, and Shine, heroes of an x-rated world. I was always amazed to hear these urban griots cite extensive passages about these heroes as they waited to be called to caddy.

Another time-killer for caddies was shooting dice. I had learned how to shoot dice from Mitchell, who showed Junie and me how to make dice out of the plentiful red clay. He also showed us how to determine if dice were fake or loaded. By the time I started caddying, I was well versed in this gambling vice. I also had sense enough not to try my luck; I caddied to make money, not lose it. Some guys, though, were so successful at shooting dice that caddying became secondary.

Caddying was like homecoming. Friends I knew from Tinbridge Hill who had moved away reappeared in my life. Their colorful personalities made caddying more of a sideshow than just bag toting. For example, no caddy could match Edward Crowder at banter and "playing the dozens." He invented colorful similes and metaphors to talk about other caddies' mothers that would have us bent over in laughter. He carried a knife that he liberally pulled out to threaten the young caddies. Once we got to know him better, we concluded his bark was much worse than his bite.

Crowder was responsible for giving Rand a new nickname. He began calling him "Rand Hunt." Why, I don't know. But over time, the name was whittled down to "Hunt," the name he is known by today.

It took two or three trips to Boonsboro before the caddy master finally called me to caddy. I think he had run out of good caddies, and he needed someone who wouldn't mind spending time in the woods tracking down the balls of whiffers, our name for duffers.

As I became better acquainted with the caddy master, my fortunes picked up. Soon I was taking two golf bags instead of one. There were certain bags caddies dreaded getting, like McWane's or Sackett's, because they felt like the cow had been attached to the leather when they made the bag. After toting these bags, I would come home after eighteen holes with depressions on my shoulder as a result of bag straps weighing me down.

The caddy fee was two dollars per bag and a fifty-cent tip if I were lucky. Veteran caddies like John, the brother of my uncle by marriage, and the legendary Skin Tom got the choicest golfers. They were assured both good tips and good drinks.

Other seasoned caddies gave us young ones vivid recollections of Skin Tom's golf prowess, pointing to some distant markers on the first tee as the unimaginable length of his drives. I used to wonder, as did others, how he would have fared if he had been given the opportunity, in his prime, to compete professionally.

My most embarrassing caddying moment came when I was assigned to caddy for one of the most pitiful whiffers at Boonsboro. We called him "Boodley-Boo" because that was the signature phrase he heralded when he arrived at the club. Although he was one of the most entertaining personalities on the links, caddies prayed not to get his bag. Caddying for Boodley Boo meant a long day on the course, made even longer with jaunts in the woods.

When he got up to the tee, I hoped that he would at least hit the ball in the fairway. No such luck. I had placed myself down the hill near the woods away from the tee box to get a better look at where he would be hitting. He swung at the ball much like a lumberjack cutting wood. His ball hooked to the rough, about fifty yards from the tee box, forewarning me that I would be on the course for the long haul.

After spotting his ball, I watched as he whacked it into the fairway. Then, on the next shot, he hit it into the woods. Junie and I went into the woods to search for the ball, which was presumed lost. After about five minutes of searching, I came across it, proudly saying, "I found it."

Boodley Boo came to the spot and decided to play the ball. He looked around and asked, "Where are my clubs?" I looked around and didn't see them. Not only did I not see them, I couldn't remember where I had left them. My body flushed as I tried to retrace my steps. Blank. My mind was empty. Desperate, I weaved in and out of the woods for another five minutes before I shouted with relief, "I found them."

This incident heightened one of my greatest fears: forgetfulness. My mother had told me that a doctor described me as having an overactive mind. Whether or not forgetfulness was symptomatic of this condition, I knew that failing to remember got me in more trouble than some of my deliberate mischief.

The opportunity to play golf free was the biggest perk of caddying. Monday was caddy day, and to be eligible to use the golf course, all it took was to caddy one time. Caddies were the only blacks allowed to play at Boonsboro, since the club had a "Whites Only" membership policy.

Playing golf on Mondays was more of an outing than hitting a ball around the course. None of us had a full set of clubs, so we shared. Our used canvas golf bags, bought at the caddy shack, could barely hold the assortment of second-hand clubs we owned. Even as we pooled our clubs, we rarely had enough variety to be legally called a set. All our golf balls came from foraging through the woods looking for the errant projectiles. We became quite adept in distinguishing golf balls from forest flora like mushrooms or flowers.

To complement our golf outing, we would pack an assortment of treats and look forward to our traditional picnic on the fourteenth green, which was across from Mitchell's Store on Boonsboro Road. We knew the name Mitchell carried a lot of weight in this area of Bedford County, and we did not want to get tangled up into any incident that would land us in the jail operated by Sheriff Mitchell. Sometimes we would go into the store and buy soft drinks, crackers, or an egg salad sandwich. Once our bellies were full, we resumed play.

One day a group of us, including Boodie, Bones, Shine, and Ba'y Bro (often called "Cheese"), made our usual stop on the fourteenth hole. Shine went to Mitchell's Store as we sat around eating and practiced putting on the green. Suddenly we heard a crackling through the woods and saw Shine, bug-eyed, running along one of the paths, carrying a six-pack of soft drinks. "They saw me," he said, hiding the drinks in the bushes. Then he disappeared into the woods along the fifteenth fairway. In a few minutes a displeased white man burst through the path. "Did you see a boy run through here?" he asked.

With feigned innocence, we all professed no knowledge of having seen Shine. He looked around at us to see if any of us fit the description, then said that Shine had stolen some drinks from his store. We shrugged, but he was too upset to sense that we were lying.

He took a perfunctory look around before deciding to return to his store. Shine never returned, so we concluded that there was no need to leave the soft drinks to be damaged by the elements. When the coast was clear, we took the soft drinks and added them to our feast.

When we caught up with Shine later that day, he told us how frightened he was of getting caught. To eliminate any future suspicion regarding young black boys stealing from Mitchell's Store, we avoided returning to the scene of the crime.

Since playing golf was free, we sometimes played two rounds if we could maintain our energy. Many of our golf lessons came from observing the golfers and coaching ourselves as we knocked severely damaged balls into the woods on Tinbridge Hill.

By the time I was fifteen, I had retired both from playing golf, which I never was too good at, and from caddying, at which I thought I could hold my own if only I could remember where I would leave my golfer's bag.

Golf was not the only sport to which I got my first exposure at the dead-end of McKinley Street. Someone had erected a crude basketball goal where the street stopped and dropped in elevation, becoming a small plot of land formerly used as a vegetable garden. The goal was only about six feet high, and the ground was as lumpy as a plowed field. The basketballs we used were from another era. They had inner tubes and laces, making dribbling even more difficult on the rough ground. The unchallenging low goal made Junie and me seek better playing conditions.

The nurses' quarters behind the hospital had a recreational area shielded by the hedges opposite the Wall. Besides a tennis court, where we never ventured, it contained a basketball court on the grass. For a few brief encounters, we played hassle free. Then one day we were told we couldn't use the area anymore because we were wearing out the lawn.

We thought that if you put a basketball court on grass, you should expect wear and tear. Of course, we never expressed these sentiments. We stopped playing as instructed and never saw anyone else play on the basketball court, making us continue to wonder why the goal had been built in the first place. And we couldn't stop wondering whether the fact that two black boys were having fun, at nobody's expense, had anything to do with the decision.

As we got older, we began to go to Yoder School to play. Soon I got my first basketball for Christmas, a rubber one that bounced like Flubber. Because other boys my age and I were considered too young to play with the big guys, we would shoot around while they played the whole court. If my basketball strayed onto the court, they would sling it down the hill or try to kick it to Second Street. Humiliated, I'd retrieve my ball, which the big guys called a balloon, and wait until they left in order to shoot around without interference.

My obsession with basketball saw no limits. In the seventh grade, my diminutive classmate Melvin Pollard and I met one overcast day after school to play one on one. I had a decided height advantage on Melvin, but he was determined to beat me. Before the first game ended, the overcast turned to rain. Soon we found ourselves battling both each other and the rain. Each game I won seemed to make Melvin more determined to win. I wanted to go home, but he insisted we continue to play. I acceded and played until he finally won a game. By that time we had played so many games that neither one of us went home with a dry spot on our clothes. As I walked home, my PF Flyers feeling like wet sponges beneath my feet, I questioned my sanity. I was glad that no one was home when I arrived; if so, Melvin wouldn't have been the only one to beat me.

Ms. Anderson's seventh grade class had some veteran students who had been retained a year, including Willie Calloway and Lawrence Perkins. They complemented the Yoder School intramural basketball team that won the elementary school championship game. I considered them superior athletes and didn't think I was old enough to play on their level.

All that changed as I discovered, as did some of my basketball-playing friends, that I could jump quicker and higher than most guys in our neighborhood. My shooting was pitiful, though I sometimes had flashes of brilliance. While my basketball-playing friends, like Boodie, Ben, Wee Wee, William "Bud" Harvey, Elwood "Skeeter" Hartman, Robert "Sonny" Tanner, Lee Stevens, and Albert Eubanks, made the Jay Vee and varsity teams, I elected to remain a playground ballplayer, due to a lack of confidence and extreme self-consciousness.

Up in Smoke

When I was ten years old, I got hooked on smoking. Not just cigarettes, but anything that could make ashes and spew forth carbon. It seems that I blame Mitchell McCoy for all my vices, and since I'm on a roll, I'll also give him some of the credit for this one.

In the fall of 1954, when the weeds and plants had dried out, I met Mitchell and Junie near the billboard bordering Junie's yard. They had harvested some dried twigs with hollow piths, which they had lit. When a red ash formed, they put the twigs to their mouths, inhaled, and blew out smoke.

The closest I had ever come to smoking involved blowing the dust off candy cigarettes and the powder from the fake ones we bought at Hayslett's store. Without hesitation, I fired up a twig and puffed.

Mitchell showed me the art of regular and French inhaling. I was officially cool. Next we graduated to real cigarettes. In his store, Mr. Phillips often sold loose cigarettes for two cents apiece. We would sometimes need a note from an adult before he sold one to us. We seldom had the luxury of buying cigarettes, so we would scavenge cigarette butts from ashtrays, or, if desperate enough—which I often found myself—pick them off the sidewalk, with total disregard as to their origin.

Mitchell also exposed me to loose Prince Albert tobacco and Bugler and OCB cigarette papers. I ineptly rolled cigarettes in the manner I had seen some of my favorite cowboys do in the B-westerns, but my end product was tattered paper, with strands of tobacco dangling from both ends as if trying to escape their impending date with a match. In the end, rolling cigarettes caused me to ingest more tobacco than I smoked.

One other thing Mitchell showed me was how to grasp a lit cigarette in the fold of the tongue, insert it in the mouth, blow out smoke to prove it was still lit, and then return it to the lips unaided by hands. I had seen this maneuver done in the movies and was eager to give it a try. Without practicing, I took a lit cigarette butt, placed it on my tongue, and retracted the cigarette into my mouth…where it fell. Palate and tongue blistered as I spat the now soggy, half-lit cigarette from my mouth. Another inaugural effort fumbled. Once my mouth healed, I practiced privately with unlit cigarettes. Though I was successful at practice, I abided by my own adage— "Once burned, twice shy"— and never attempted this stunt "live" again.

By the fifth grade, Junie and I knew every major cigarette brand and the cities and companies that made them. We had experimented with following brands: Chesterfield, Old Gold, Pall Mall, Lucky Strike, Camel, Kool, Viceroy, Winston, Salem, Philip Morris, Marlboro, and Parliament. Then one day Junie and I decided to quit because of information that linked cigarettes with lung cancer; however, this was not the end of my smoking habit.

I had stopped smoking through the sixth grade, but in the seventh grade, and with a lot of free time on my hands during my after-school hours, I discovered a cheap source of smoke: newspapers. My prepubescent brain made a mockery of common sense. I began to tear up newspapers into cigarette-sized strips, roll them up tightly, and smoke them just as I had the twigs.

My obsession with polluting my lungs with carbon caused me to take desperate measures. When I ran out of newspaper, I would resort to brown paper bags. When I ran out of matches, I would turn on the oven and light my ersatz cigarettes from the red-hot coils. I knew that this was abnormal behavior, but this addictive vice was cheap and easy. I needed something to bring me back to reality, which is what the brown paper bag did.

Out of greed, I rolled the brown paper until it became cigar-sized. After I blew out the flame, a huge red ash formed at the tip. Determined to supersaturate my lungs, I inhaled the smoldering ashes like a vacuum. Instead of smoke, the air re-ignited the flames, causing me to suck in fire. I could not exhale fast enough, and since we had no running water in the house, I had no way of soothing my literally parched throat. Then something kicked into my head, redirecting my neural pathways from obsessive stupidity to sober logic.

I quit smoking, this time for good. Well, at least until the summer of 1960, when, during my last year of caddying, I took up smoking Kent cigarettes to ward off gnats. Once my caddying days ended, so did my desire to smoke.

Race and Other Relations

G radations of skin color, being an instantly recognizable human difference, became part of our early conversations regarding race. Most of my friends were light-skinned. My skin fell into the medium brown range, yet I was one of the darkest children in the neighborhood. With the exceptions of the Johnsons and our family, most children in our neighborhood had lighter than average "black" skin. We discussed and acknowledged our differences, but skin color had no bearing on our associations with each other.

Because of the structure of our society and its emphasis on color, we found ourselves being resented by the adults among our nearest white neighbors, who had to come to grips with living side-by-side with or in close proximity to black families. When Junie and his family moved to McIvor Street, they encroached on the part of the street inhabited by whites. The Scott family probably received more tolerance because of their light skin than my dark-skinned family would have if we had traded places. Still, race relations were strained by the then-current social mores.

Contrary to adult animosity, black and white children played well together when given an opportunity. Ann, a white girl about my age, played with us, oblivious to our racial stratification. We knew, though, that our social arenas were different, especially since Jim Crow signs and practices relegated where we could eat, sleep, be entertained, and be educated.

I liked playing with Ann, who lived two houses from the Scotts, and we often wound up in the strawberry patch across from her house, where we would pick the fruit undetected by the elderly Mrs. DePriest, who owned the plot. One day, when we were about ten, her father called her into the house as we played in the strawberry patch. That would be the last time she would speak to me.

I imagine that her father preached to her the facts of life regarding black and white relationships and gave her certain rules she had to obey. When I saw her in the yard after he called her in, I asked her if she could play. Then I saw a frightened and confused look on her face as she remained silent. I asked her if there was anything wrong, but she faded through their side door, and I never saw her again.

Although I was confused, I was not stupid. I knew that we lived in two different worlds; I just did not know why it had to be this way. I could adjust to discrimination because it came with being black; however, I often wondered how Ann felt when she was told that she could not play with her friends, not because of some character flaw, but solely because my melanin was more active than hers.

Cutchie told me that the same "facts of white life" had faced Mike and Kent, who lived next to the McCoys. They were called into the house, received their white rites-of-passage sermon, and forever afterward distanced themselves from their darker friends. Even today, people continue to let color gradation, found in a layer of skin about as thick as this sheet of paper, be a source of illogical, unmerited, and unwarranted attacks on fellow human beings.

One of the most frightening racial incidents I remember came at night as Junie, Rand, and I were returning from the Harrison Theater, the only black movie house in the city. Junie had purchased a peashooter, and as we walked down Federal Street, just past Second, he blew a pea at a car that was heading towards Fifth Street.

The car stopped in front of the Hoyle-Halsey house, which we referred to as the John Lynch house, and two white boys, much larger and older than we were, emerged, accusing us of throwing rocks at the car. We decided not to stay around to debate and took off down the street, with them in hot pursuit.

Rand and I sprinted around the corner at First Street, where we thought the pursuit might end, since we had now entered the all-black section of Tinbridge Hill. We had barely hidden under a car opposite where George Williams lived when we heard Junie's footsteps.

We could hear him breathing heavily, as the bitter white boys tried to trap him around the car. We saw his feet run one way, then reverse directions, with the pursuers on his heels. Then, through an evasive move, he took off towards Jackson Street, with the boys still chasing him.

After they left our hiding place, Rand and I retreated towards Federal Street to the safety of our neighborhood, wondering once again if Junie had been able to get away. Soon we would have our answer, as Junie reappeared, triumphant and unscathed. Once more Junie's pluck had saved him from a situation that shouldn't have occurred in the first place.

Not all contact with whites produced negative results. When I was about nine, the Brooks brothers moved next to Hayslett's Store. The two white boys became instant friends for all of us little black boys to share.

Although I don't remember the parents, they had to have a certain amount of tolerance to let us come into their house and take the brothers on our fun-filled excursions. The first time we went skating together, one of the brothers—Sonny, I think—had his skates to slip from under him, causing him to land on the back of his head. With the sound of the thud, no one laughed. He grabbed his head as he moaned, while I thought that we were going to lose an opportunity to bond. But he recovered, and we skated cheerfully down Federal Street.

Another time our playing with the Brooks brothers stopped my heart was when we journeyed to the ridges on McIvor Street. We had selected vines on which to swing out over the trees below. Sonny, as daring as anyone, got a running start and swung out to a point that had to be a forty-foot drop.

As we watched Sonny swing into no man's land, we heard the crackling of branches as the vine snapped and saw him freefalling to his death. My mouth was agape as Sonny's life flashed before me. Fortunately, hickory trees grew tall on that hillside, and he landed in the top of one. We all breathed a collective sigh of relief as Sonny made his way down his tree of life.

Our friendships with the Brooks brothers ended when they moved away. Although we never forged strong bonds, my memory of having them as friends has never weakened.

On Federal Street between First and Hollins stood three establishments operated by whites. Each proprietor lived above the store where business was conducted. Cochran's Store, occupying the corner of First and Federal, was a three-story building with the story below street level considered a basement.

Mrs. Cochran was an elderly lady who sold candy that was as old as she was. Her store had passed its heyday and opened infrequently. In the back of her deeply recessed yard rose a black-heart cherry tree that grew up to the sidewalk, just beyond the reaches of prepubescent fingers. No matter how hard we tried, we could not reel in branches to sample what we imagined to be the tastiest cherries in the neighborhood.

On rare occasions, we tried to take advantage of Mrs. Cochran's poor eyesight by passing off slugs as money. Most of the time this scam failed, but sometimes, I believe out of sympathy, she allowed us to get a nickel's worth of her vintage candy or ginger snaps.

Phillips' Coffee Shop was situated across from the hospital and catered mostly to the nurses and other medical staff. Mr. Phillips seldom had dry goods, but he did have a few emergency items that, occasionally, I was sent to buy. He sometimes opened packages and sold items individually, even though this practice was illegal.

Sometimes I was sent to the store to purchase individual feminine products. Such a transaction contained an aura of secrecy worthy of a Hollywood cloak-and-dagger plot. I was given a hand-written note stating what I was to purchase. I never said a word. Mr. Phillips would bend below his counter and put the item in a brown paper bag, concealing it from my view. He would then instruct me not to look in the bag. I would pay for the item and head home. I never figured out the big deal behind this purchase, because I always read the note, and I always looked.

When Lynchburg General Hospital moved, the main source of Mr. Phillips' business moved with it. He managed to stay open a few months longer, but he soon closed his store and moved away.

The owner of Hayslett's Store personified true racial hostility. Located at 86 Federal Street, about a house-length from Cochran's Store, it had two floors below street level. Mr. Hayslett was caught between his hatred of blacks and his economic dependency on the very people he detested. His wife and daughter appeared to be more tolerant and didn't seem to have the same sentiment that he harbored regarding blacks.

Each time I went into the store I sensed resentment. Mr. Hayslett showed his contempt for his black patrons, though I don't know if it was his personality or a deep-seated racism that caused him to disrespect us. His store contained canned goods, bulk cold cuts, kerosene, and other products we needed until we could do serious grocery shopping at Bibee's

Supermarket, located near the corner of Fifth and Federal streets.

My worst experience at Hayslett's Store came when Momma sent me to get a can of vegetables, with specific instructions to have it put in a paper bag. I took my nine-year-old self to the store and, upon paying for the item, requested a bag. Instead of honoring my request, Mr. Hayslett flew into a tirade. "What do you need a bag for?" he snapped. Then he took the can and dropped it on the counter. "See? If you drop it, it ain't gonna hurt nothing." I saw a small dent form in the corner of the can as he continued. "You just want to get a free bag to put your lunch in. Now take this can and go home."

Shocked and humiliated, I walked up the two steps of this recessed store and exited with my head down. When I told Momma what had happened, she scolded me for not following her instructions and then went back to Hayslett's to take care of business. From that point on, I never had any problems getting a bag from Mr. Hayslett; seldom do I now purchase items, no matter how small, without requesting a bag.

With the closing of Cochran's and Phillips' stores, Mr. Hayslett maintained a monopoly on serving the community with goods and bile. Around 1957, the landscape changed. The McGraws bought and reopened Cochran's Store and brought something to the business side of Federal Street that had been missing: compassion.

The McGraws sold food and used furniture. They knew how to talk to their customers, and sometimes Mrs. McGraw would have extended conversations with me, a rarity considering I was still a reticent thirteen-year-old.

Momma conducted a lot of business with them, buying pieces of inexpensive furniture that they sold. Momma also recognized that the furniture they sold, though cheap, was of high quality, so she tried to buy up as much as she could before the McGraws realized their mistake.

Although the McGraws had established good race relations with blacks, not all of their patrons did the same. When I was twelve and master of my skates, I had to run an errand for Momma to McGraw's Store. Standing on the corner as I skated toward the store were three or four white youths around my age. As I approached them, I could sense they had mischief on their minds.

My mother bought this walnut hall rack from the McGraws for fifteen dollars.

One of the observations blacks made about confrontations with white males was that they seldom instigated trouble when in one-on-one situations, but when they were in a group, then they could show their "bravery."

Mentally, I was prepared to do battle, but my skates were a chink in my defensive armor. As I got closer to the store, I tried to ignore the boys, but one of them tried to trip me as I skated past him. I avoided his foot and skated off the sidewalk into the grass. There I challenged him, but he and the others laughed as I put up my dukes.

They uttered a few snide remarks as I took off my skates, placing them on the top steps of the entrance to the store. Mrs. McGraw saw what had happened and gave me a few encouraging words as I paid for my items. As she was bagging them, one of the boys took my skates and began skating in front of the store, although he hadn't strapped them down. I hurried out of the store and retrieved my skates, while they taunted and threatened me.

Again I put up my dukes, fuming with anger and wanting to spew venom out of my mouth. To my dissatisfaction, when I spoke this time, I sounded like a little sissy, and my mannerisms reflected the same. It was a moment I could not pull back. I wanted to express my toughness, but my voice and body betrayed me. I wanted to kick myself for coming off so weak. Still, I was prepared to fight any of them had it come to that. I also wished that I could have caught one of them alone, to see how bad he really was.

I believed that some white parents went to great lengths to instill hatred in their children. One white boy, who was about five years old the year I fell down the steps in Dearington, used to throw rocks at me whenever I passed his yard, a half block from McGraw's Store and hidden by hedges. I was bold enough to chase him into his yard on several occasions and wondered why his parents would knowingly allow him to practice this malicious behavior. I considered him the meanest, rottenest boy in the neighborhood.

A few days after my accident on the Dearington steps, I was walking down Federal Street near his house when I saw him and his mother walking towards me. As I passed him, he swung his fist into my side, precisely on the spot of my bandaged wound. I winced in pain, though I did not say anything, and waited for his mother to reprimand him. She instead ignored his actions, as if to acknowledge that what he did was acceptable. If he had been by himself, I have no idea what the outcome would have been. Or maybe I do.

A testament of my response to the racism of young children occurred one Sunday when my sister and I, being about nine, were coming home from church. As we approached the corner of Second and Federal streets, two young white children, a boy about six and his sister, about four, started to agitate us with racial slurs. The boy started throwing rocks at us, and I warned him to stop. He continued, while his sister backed him up with more racist comments. Without warning, I ran across the street and chased him into what we called the John Lynch house, where he lived, and smacked him in the back as he crossed the front-door threshold. I turned around, running towards the spot where I had left my sister. As I fled down the sidewalk from the porch, the little girt was coming towards me. In her prissy manner she said, "You black b—." Before she could finish the sentence, I reflexively stuck out my hand and popped her in the mouth as I hit full stride. The next sound I heard from her was wailing. Her crying echoed through the screen door as she entered her hallway.

I have never considered myself violent and have seldom been malicious, but this incident revealed my capacity for defensive aggression when the situation warranted it. This was one of the few times I ever hit or hurt someone without feeling remorse.

Segregation strained relationships and caused us to create ways to equalize racial discrimination, particularly in the movie theaters. Although we could depend on choice seating at the Harrison, the other movies downtown and in Fort Hill limited our seating to the balconies.

We attended four theaters downtown. The Isis (which I first referred to as the "Is, Is" upon reading the name in the newspaper) would be the only theater to close in the 1950s. The Paramount, located at Fifth and Main streets across from Cary Chevrolet, was the most popular, while the Warner, at Eleventh and Main, had a certain degree of sophistication. The theater we dreaded was the Academy, which we dubbed "the Rat Hole" because rats roamed the floors of the balcony, our designated seating area.

Each of these theaters had a separate ticket office for black patrons, to ensure that we did not mix. Segregation bred some resentment in us because the projector operator frequently reduced the volume of the movie. Since the speakers were located in the "Whites Only" section, it was difficult for us to hear.

We took vengeance on white patrons by converting wire into staples that we shot from rubber bands into the theater ceiling so the staples could bounce down on those seated below. Since the ricochets changed the trajectory of our missiles, it was difficult to pinpoint their origin. Whenever we got a hit, we would snicker as a white patron sometimes looked directly above for the source or would slap their neck, thinking an insect had landed on them. We never shot at whites directly, though we often bought hard candy and tossed it down on them.

Although segregation deprived blacks of certain societal advantages, it played a role in giving us group cohesiveness, so vital in the cultural and social development of our community. I resented that segregation assumed that all black people fit into one mind-set. My experience with the people in my neighborhood, the people with whom Momma worked at the hospital, and the men for whom I caddied gave me first-hand experience with both the compassion and the insensitivity that existed in the dominant group.

I learned how to tolerate the dichotomy in the races because of my exposure at an early age to the potential of racial harmony. Seeing the diversity of behaviors in the white youth I encountered taught me that children reflected their upbringing, and, right or wrong, parents represented the foundation of their children's emotional development.

Mainstream media had attempted to condition us, as young children, to embrace the stereotypes of Buckwheat, Rochester, and Stepin' Fetchit, without seeing a balance with people like Harry Belafonte, Paul Robeson, or Canada Lee. Seldom were we mentioned in the Lynchburg newspapers unless articles contained negative elements such as a raid on a nip joint or a crime of passion. Even our Virginia history books claimed that as an enslaved people blacks received benefits such as escape from enemies, better health care, improved religion, happiness, and prosperity.

Racial stereotyping came to the forefront of my life when, in the summer of 1957, I went downtown to exchange a bicycle chain from Sears that I had purchased the day before. I had misplaced the receipt, which I thought was no big deal.

Innocently, I told a middle-aged white sales clerk that I had bought a double-link chain that I needed to exchange for a single-link one. His response was "Are you sure you didn't steal this chain and then realize that you got the wrong one?" Shocked and angered at his insinuation, I replied, "No. I bought this chain yesterday, but I got the wrong kind. All I want to do is exchange it for a single-link one. The price is the same."

"Where is your receipt?" he asked. "I left it at home." He persisted: "I think you took this chain, and now you are trying to get another one because you got the wrong kind." I seethed inside but kept my calm, saying, "I just bought it yesterday and made a mistake."

I could see disbelief in his countenance as he discussed this situation with another white male employee. After his consultation, he played his trump card: "I'm going to call Hector Strong and see what he has to say."

Hector Strong was the black truant officer, known for his ability to chase and capture juvenile delinquents. Whenever we saw his car, we put our best foot forward for fear of winding up in the Juvenile and Domestic Relations Court.

The thought of facing Mr. Strong did not intimidate me, because I knew I was right. "Go ahead," I countered. He picked up the telephone as I defiantly looked on. He faked dialing, though I wished he had called. Seeing that I was not going to run out of the store, he hung up the phone and said, "I can't make an exchange without a receipt. You bring the receipt back, and I'll make the exchange."

I thought, "You could have said that the first time, and I wouldn't have to go through this." My problem was that I had no idea what I had done with the receipt.

I walked home with the double-link chain and told Momma what had happened. Irritated by the events and frustrated by my lack of a receipt, she chastised me for being so irresponsible as we both ransacked the house. While she continued to scold me, she stumbled upon the receipt, which calmed her down.

Sighs of relief eased our tension, and I eagerly awaited the arrival of the next day. I went back to Sears with my chain and receipt, where I saw the same man who had accused me of being a thief. Sheepishly, he confessed, "Heh, heh. I'm glad you were able to find your receipt, because we had no way of proving you bought it. You're a good man."

Had I been white, I am sure that the initial dialogue I had with the Sears employee would have gone in another direction. I had come to grips with the social and economic segregation of the races, but I had a hard time coming to terms with being unjustly accused of a crime that never happened solely based on my being black.

Silently, I made the exchange and vowed that I would never shop at Sears again. I later modified my vow when Sears moved to Pittman Plaza and I decided I could not hold the store accountable for the actions of one person.

Fifth Street, the hub of black life in Lynchburg, reminded me that blacks had contributed more to civilization than stereotypical images. An assortment of businesses lined Fifth Street from Federal to Monroe streets. When blacks said that they were going on "the Block," it was taken for granted that they were going to the 900 block of Fifth Street.

In 1956, the following businesses and organizations in the 900 block of Fifth Street, east side, were listed in the City Directory: Odd Fellows Hall, Modern Beauty Shop, Braxton A1 Transfer, Order of Eastern Star Lodge, St. Luke's Lodge, West Lodge, Leander Gibson (watch repair), Harrison Theater, Parrish's Snack Bar, Ruby McDemon, Pettis Shoe Shop, Kyle Pettis (physician), George Jackson (dentist), Southern Aid Life Insurance, Abie's Café, Hutcherson Funeral Home, Mrs. Inez Roberts, City Cab, Otey Cab, and Earl's Café.

On the west side were Holiday Sales (general merchandise), Bar-B-Que Grill, Glenn's Barber Shop, L&H Music Co. (repairs), Mack's Smoke Shop, Midway Country Produce, Community Funeral Home, Amanda Hunting (rear), Lorenzo Fels, Ralph Boulware (physician), Clara Wimbush (dentist), Carey Insurance & Real Estate, Lukengus Carey (lawyer), Henry Goodwyn, Turpin & Jones Billiards, New Era Barber Shop, Reid's Pharmacy, and Greene's Barber Shop. The Sportsman's Club was located above Greene's and extended as far as the billiard hall.

A few black citizens had residences in the 800 block of Fifth Street across from Adams Motor Company; these houses took up most of the west side of the street between Federal and Jackson. An Esso station occupied the corner lot contiguous to two car dealerships, Adams and Dickerson Buick. When leaving the Harrison Theater, my friends and I would walk across the front lot of Adams and ogle the new Chrysler Corporation cars. Then we would cut across the Esso station to view the latest Buicks and GMC trucks.

September was a highly anticipated month because we could get to see the unveiling of the new line of cars. Sometimes the vehicles would be in the

J. R. Brown Esso Servicenter at Fifth and Federal streets

Wilson Funeral Home at 808 Fifth Street, bordered by private residences

Hutcherson Funeral Home at 916 Fifth Street

The Kentucky Hotel (left) housed several fraternal organizations. The Harrison Theater is to the right of the hotel.

The Harrison Theater and surrounding businesses

Fifth and Polk streets, the most popular corner in the black community. Shown from right to left are Earl's Café, including its two-story section; City Cab and Otey Cab; Hutcherson Funeral Home; and Abie's Café (partial view).

Earl's Café. The four short stools were designed to accommodate small children.

View of Fifth Street facing north at the fork near Monroe Street and Park Avenue. The billboard hides Harper's store and the Elks Rest home.

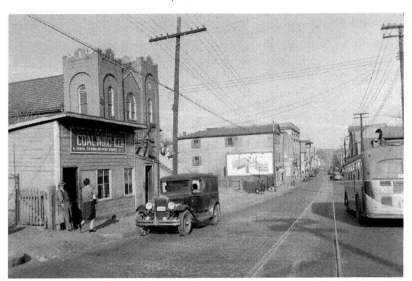

Fifth Street, looking north, near Monroe Street. The Franklin Coal Company is alongside Fifth Street Baptist Church. The building behind the billboard, at the corner of Fifth and Polk, was razed around 1951. Dr. Walter Johnson built his office there in 1952 and shortly afterward opened the Teenage Canteen in the same building.

showroom prior to their release date, and the dealers would cover their display windows with paper to make sure no one got an early peek. If we were lucky, we discovered an opening between the sheets of brown paper and got a glimpse of cars we could only dream about. Because of our proximity to these dealerships, in addition to the Hoskins Pontiac dealership at Fifth and Monroe and Cary Chevrolet at Fifth and Main, we got earlier exposure to the evolution of automobiles than some of our friends from other parts of town. On rare occasions we were bold enough to go inside the showroom to get a look at the new models, but somehow proximity negated the mystique of seeing the cars from the other side of the glass.

Adams Motor Company would eventually purchase most of the property in the 800 block of Fifth Street to expand its dealership. This transaction also meant the reduction of part of our history, as we saw Wilson's Funeral Home and the adjacent residential property razed in the name of economic progress.

On the weekends, Fifth Street blossomed, as blacks from the city and surrounding counties converged on the mecca of local black life. I watched the area transform as Reid's Pharmacy, once situated under the Douglass Hotel, relocated under the Sportsman's Club, the most vibrant entertainment venue on Fifth Street. The Elks Club catered to a more sophisticated crowd, while the Sportsman's Club offered a retreat for more down-to-earth folks. Haskins' Barber Shop, also located under the Sportsman's Club, was later converted to a pool hall.

The Harrison Theater was our ticket to the hustle and bustle of Fifth Street. Though the theater seldom afforded us an opportunity for first-release movies, it added to the personality of black life. When I paid admission to the Harrison, my scrawny size gave me an advantage at the ticket office. My sister's friend, Edna Featherstone, was a ticket seller, and until she was told I was fourteen, I continued to pay the children's price, which had increased to fifteen cents, two years past the cut-off age.

One local icon at the movie was the blind man who stood at the entrance with a cup and cane and uttered his patented phrase: "Please help me I'm blind." It was hard to avoid him, because he was positioned next to where we had to buy our tickets, and he could hear the exchange of coins. Occasionally, I would drop the penny change from my nine-cent fare. This practice-become-tradition occurred less frequently when it was rumored that he spent the money on beer at the tavern next door.

Fifth Street was the place where I found my first windfall. I was leaving Pettis' Shoe Shop, next to the Harrison Theater, when I spotted a green piece of paper that made my eyes bulge. Lying in the street near the curb down from Glenn's Barber Shop was a dollar bill. I quickly looked up and down the street before refocusing on the dollar and then ran to the site, scooping up more money than I had ever found in my life. I kept thinking someone was going to claim my find before I got out of sight, but this fear abated once I slipped the dollar into my pocket undetected. I felt like a millionaire at ten years old. I told Momma of my good fortune, and she advised me to put it in my bank. I kept the dollar for a while, but the prodigal son in me could not resist the temptation to spend it on comic books and candy. I had not earned this money, so why should I save it? I rationalized.

Fifth Street, for once, had paid me dividends. Now I was able to enjoy "the good life" without guilt. The thrill of finding this dollar gave me a taste of fleeting wealth, which I tried to take in stride. Yet for a long while, each time I went on Fifth Street, I returned to that fortuitous spot, hoping another dollar would materialize. When I began to recognize I was battling extreme odds, my Pavlovian conditioning faded and I returned to the reality of being economically impoverished.

The Harrison Theater provided a backdrop for my early existential and metacognitive thinking. As I entered my teens, I found myself frequently going to the movies alone. Walking home on Federal Street at night meant confronting demons of the dark. Several vacant lots had overhanging bushes and trees that blocked out the streetlights. If I had attended a horror movie, then these areas became ideal spots to be attacked by the Werewolf, Frankenstein, or Dracula.

To distract myself from these thoughts, I began to count my steps, then would pick out a groove in the sidewalk and estimate how many steps it would take me to reach it, or guess which foot would land closest to my target. This activity continued until I began to look at each step as a journey and formulated my first juvenile aphorism: "Every step is a future." I would say this repeatedly as I walked through the dark shadows. Even now I tend to refer to this statement as I contemplate the meaning of my life.

Metacognition, an esoteric word bandied around educational and psychological circles, represents a person's ability to predict their abilities and monitor mastery of them. Once I discovered I had a slightly better-than-average jumping ability, I used to target leaves high on trees as I traveled to and from the theater, to see if I could grab them. Sometimes I would set my goal to a height just beyond my reach, yet when I jumped, I amazed myself by plucking what I thought was the unattainable. Later in life I would realize that if I could keep my goals just beyond my reach, I might continue to amaze myself.

Strained race relations continued to interfere with our developmental potential. Segregation, though it represented a blight on social, cultural, and economic progress, gave blacks in Lynchburg a common bond and helped us forge an identity as we lived through difficult times. Segregation led to our homogeneity as a people, though we, like whites, had social strata. We developed leaders and people with character and commitment yet also had a seamy element, just as whites did, as evidenced by some who made frequent visits to the "red light" district on Fourth Street.

I can only speculate on the impact and progress our city would have made had the white power structure been more visionary and less absorbed in ancestor worship. Maybe if we had authentic social interaction, then we could all see that to reach a higher level of growth and development, we have to imagine ourselves at the base of the steps in Dearington. We all seek to reach the top and climb the steps from our different vantage points. Although we may take different paths and proceed at different rates, we will often reach a step at the same time. In doing so, we can acknowledge that we are on the same level and can continue our journey to the top. And if we should tumble to the bottom, as I did, may we have someone like Mr. Martin to pick us up, nurse our wounds, and help us on our journey.

Once we reach the top, then we will be able to marvel at our individual journeys yet realize that we all have reached the same destination. In this way, we can appreciate each other and have a better understanding of what it takes for us to be fully human. Then maybe we can see problems from different perspectives and make sense of the words of Albert Einstein: "Problems cannot be solved at the level of consciousness that created them."

Crime and Punishment

My wandering mind contributed to the punishments I received growing up. My patented answer to Momma's probing into why I failed to do a task or be somewhere was "I forgot." This answer found no sympathy with her; instead, it doomed me to honor her request to get a switch from the privet hedge that grew in abundance between our yard and the DeLoatches'.

My first severe punishment resulted from my fascination with fire. In the winter of 1951, my seven-year-old mind marveled alone, watching the flickering flames in the small tin stove in our boys' bedroom weave patterns on the embers. To enhance the visual effect, I would place newspaper in the stove and watch it smolder until it reached its kindling point before bursting into flames. Then I would watch the fleeting vestiges of red dots weave through the paper, transforming any remaining traces of paper to carbon.

Like some mad scientist, I kept experimenting with paper, trying to guess how close I could get to it before it burst into flames. Each time I conducted this experiment, I grew bolder and added more paper. Then I finally reached my limit. I placed one piece of paper too many onto the fire, and, before I could realize what had happened, flames jumped out of the stove onto the floor.

Immediate panic engulfed me as I tried to figure out what to do. Surely I would be punished for playing in fire if I called out. So I sat there as flames danced around the stove until someone downstairs smelled smoke. Momma and Joe, a man who temporarily stayed with us, rushed upstairs to see me paralyzed as the flames crackled between the stove and me.

Joe smothered the flames, while Momma rescued me. "Why didn't you tell somebody the house was on fire?" she said, looking at me like the idiot I was. I had no explanation as she prepared to inflict punishment. But in a surprise move, Joe volunteered to whip my behind, which he did. I didn't mind the whipping so much as I resented who administered it. He wasn't part of our family, so I didn't think he had the right to whip me. Whippings were reserved for my father, who never laid a hand on me, and my mother, who did. To have Joe whip me marked the first and last time I was whipped by anyone other than my mother.

Failing to follow her instructions one day in the summer of 1955, when I was ten, gave Momma just cause to exact punishment from me, when I thought my mischief had gone undetected. She was going to visit Ms. McIvor and asked me to close the Venetian blinds to my bedroom. True to form, I forgot to follow her instructions, preferring instead to concentrate on my diving techniques.

Visualizing myself as the next Jimmy Brown on the Jefferson Park diving board, I dove on my bed using a variety of flips and twists, bouncing safely and straining the slats under the mattress. I had broken slats before when bouncing on the bed with Billie, but by itself my light weight posed no danger of repeating the previous damage. My diving routine continued for about fifteen minutes—unbeknownst to me, under the watchful eye of Momma and Ms. McIvor, who could see my every move through the window, whose blinds I had forgotten to close.

In the midst of a somersault, the unexpected happened. Momma appeared at the top of the stairs at the curtained entrance to my bedroom. Before I could gather myself, she grabbed the first thing on which she could put her hands—ironically, a rubber swim fin—and commenced to whack me across my bottom.

Fortunately for me, the frog fin, as menacing as it appeared, provided little pain as a tool of punishment. I tried to fake agony, but Momma was wise to my act. Unfortunately for me, one of my belts was in plain sight. She grabbed it and whaled the daylights out of me until real tears streamed down my face.

After exhausting all her energy and satisfying herself that the embarrassment I had caused had received retribution, she said triumphantly, "You'll think twice the next time I ask you to do something." After whipping me, and, to my mind, leaving me on the floor for dead, she returned to Ms. McIvor. I, on the other hand, crawled under the bed seeking sanctuary for my wounds. I knew Momma and Ms. McIvor were getting a good laugh at my expense, so I lay amid dust bunnies, plotting my future.

"I will run away," I thought. "No, I can't do that because I have no place to go. I'll make her think I ran away. I'm going to stay under this bed so long that she will think I left." So I remained hidden under the bed, playing with dust bunnies, inspecting slats, and counting bedsprings. I waited and waited, but no one came to check on me. Frustrated, I slid from under the bed and dusted myself off.

I closed the shades, regretting that I had forgotten to obey Momma. Never again did I use the bed as my diving pool, and never again did I fail to close the blinds without prompting.

Junie contributed to a significant proportion of my punishments, though I accept full responsibility for my actions. I had just turned twelve and, in the tradition of the Baptist church, was slated for what I considered a primitive rite of passage, a sort of Bar Mitzvah without the grueling task of memorizing the haftarah. What I had to endure was the ritual of Christian conversion, where I, along with other candidates in our church, sat on the

Fifth Street Baptist Church Choir with Rev. Harvey Stevens

front row and waited for the Spirit to hit us so we could qualify for baptism.

The choir sang hymns as this group of pre-teens, overwhelmed by the magnitude of the event, sat passively on the pew. Then one of the church ladies, who I think had a self-appointed role as conversion-encourager, prodded us one by one to get up and accept our fate as candidates for baptism. The first time she poked me, saying "Get on up there," I looked at her with discomfort and disdain.

I continued to wait for the Spirit, but the prodder lost patience, practically scooping me out of my seat. I got up mainly to keep her from putting her hands on me, but my action was taken as a sign that the Spirit had reached me.

As I awaited baptism, which was going to be a couple of weeks away, I committed my first public crime. Sometimes when we—Bill, Paul, Rand, Junie, and I—left the Harrison Theater, nightfall had already blanketed the city. On Harrison Street between Fourth and Fifth was a small scrap-metal yard, where we often scavenged for valueless slats of aluminum that we converted into swords.

Junie told me of the plan to take our scavenging to the next level. Under the guidance of Bill, we agreed to use the cover of darkness to take whatever iron we could pilfer from the yard because we knew it could fetch us a tidy sum at the Foundry.

Stealthily, we rounded the corner at Fifth and Harrison. In less than a minute, we descended upon the target area, loading our arms with as much iron as we could carry. As I struggled to pick up a weight to carry, all my friends vanished through the trees lining Harrison Street, heading home. I lifted the heavy metal in my arms, and as soon as I turned around, the spotlight on a police car that had just arrived on the scene blinded me.

Quickly, two white policemen got out of the car as I stood petrified. Everyone else had gotten away, but when they saw that I was caught, with their loyalty at stake, they returned and surrendered their loot. Being captured caused me to flash all kinds of horrid scenes in my head: reform school, jail, and worse—Momma!

The police got out their pads and recorded our names. I was doomed. There was no way we were going to get out of this. All of us, individually, considered giving the wrong names and addresses, but we knew that would make matters worse. Surprisingly, the police treated us as the misguided youth we were, as opposed to hardened delinquents. They never raised their voices, passed judgment, or taunted us. They had caught us red-handed, so there was no reason to rub salt in our delinquent wounds. After the police finished writing, they told us that we would have to appear before Hector Strong. Suddenly the butterflies in my stomach felt more like buzzards.

We walked home like battle-weary soldiers. "Why didn't you run when you saw the police?" I was asked. "I didn't see them until it was too late," I responded. We knew that each of us had to face the music and the wrath of parents. We collaborated on how to soften the blow, agreeing that we would all tell the same story: that we considered the scrap iron in the same category as the aluminum. Since we had previously asked for and received permission to take the aluminum, we felt the same applied to the scrap iron. This story was our saving grace.

Momma was particularly incensed, especially since I had just been converted. I received my just desserts—a switchful of whipping—even after telling her our rationale for the thievery.

At the appointed hour, our bungling band of burglars, escorted by displeased parents, marched to Mr. Strong's office. He listened sympathetically to our pleas, and since none of us had been in prior trouble, we escaped with a warning. We emphatically promised that he would not have to worry about us getting into any more trouble, and we left his office without the weight of the world on our shoulders.

I had stayed out of trouble for over a year when once again Junie became a catalyst. This time, though, I had a trifecta going for me. I was supposed to play trumpet in a music recital at Armstrong Elementary School one Saturday in the spring of 1957 and was to meet Momma downtown to buy some clothes for the event. That day I went down in the woods with my friends and forgot about the time and the events of the evening.

On our return from the woods, Junie told me that his white neighbor next door had a cherry tree that grew next to a fence on the hillside above Hollins Mill Road. He said that the day before, he had climbed the hill and picked cherries undetected. He laid out a plan for me to repeat this strategy and come away with the off-limits fruit.

I went to Junie's house, where I told one of his younger sisters, Sarah, of my plan. She agreed to accompany me on this caper. As planned, we left their unfenced yard, which sloped down to Hollins Mill Road, and climbed up the bank where the cherries awaited us. And so did the neighbor.

Before we could pick one cherry, our plans were foiled. He must have been watching us from the time we left the yard until we got within reach of the cherries. Once discovered, we made a hasty retreat. Unfortunately, Sarah couldn't escape far, since she lived next door. I fled, thinking that I had evaded the neighbor, only to find out how nasty he really was. He found out where I lived and called the police, who arrived at my house before I did.

Momma was infuriated. First, she had waited downtown for over an hour, then I had forgotten about the music recital, and now this—the police coming to our house because I had attempted to steal some cherries. She scolded me in her worst intonations, got me ready for my seven o'clock engagement, and called a cab, since it was too late for me to take the bus.

After the music recital, which would have gone on perfectly well without my minor input, I returned home and heard little about retribution or punishment. I thought if I could get into the bed undetected, then Momma's anger would subside by morning, and my punishment would decrease proportionately.

While Momma was downstairs, I rushed to get out of my clothes and into my pajamas. Momma's intuition must have been at its peak, for as soon as I came out of my underwear and began to step my naked behind into my pajamas, she appeared like a freight train roaring through the tunnel below us. Armed with the thickest switches I had ever seen, she unleashed a barrage of lashes, not fit for man or beast—just a miscreant little boy. I tried to dive under the bed, but those switches with Medusa-like tentacles snapped at my bare flesh as Momma dragged me into her whipping zone.

All I can remember hearing between my sobs and wails, which I knew everybody on the street heard, was Momma saying, "Didn't I tell you…!" Each time I thought she would lighten up, Momma shifted gears and the switch obeyed, bending, but not breaking. None too soon, the whipping ceased, and I lay sobbing in exhaustion. This was not one of those "This is going to hurt me worse than it's going to hurt you" whippings. This was "Vengeance is mine!"

I examined my wounds, picking at the welts and trying to make them bleed in an effort to drum up sympathy, thinking that if Momma saw blood, she might think twice about whipping me so viciously the next time. But the pain of aggravating my wounds was too great, and I resigned to letting the welts remain as evidence of my misdeeds.

I had just suffered miserably for crimes that I thought were minor: I had forgotten; I had attempted to steal cherries. How criminal were these acts? Yes, I had messed up, but the whipping of a lifetime? Did I deserve this? Then I thought to put myself in Momma's shoes. How much did her blood boil as she waited downtown on the corner of Ninth and Main while I gallivanted and traipsed through the woods? How irritated and inconvenienced was she to have to fork up extra money for a cab? How embarrassing was it to have the police to come to her house, regardless of how minor the offense, when neighbors could interpret this as a serious event? If I had been Momma, I would have whipped me severely, too.

By the time I was fourteen, my whippings were behind me. I had stopped most of my youthful mischief, though one more little blast awaited me. And yes, Junie was the catalyst for my final punishment.

Though I have blocked from memory the actual exchange of words, this I do remember: Junie had come to my house to accompany me somewhere. As Momma walked from our front room to the kitchen, she asked me about our plans. To show off for Junie, I made my first and last smart-alecky remark to her.

The next thing I remember happening was the pop of Momma's backhand against my lips and a warning never to smart-talk her again. This was the first time she had ever hit me in the face, and the shock of getting smacked at a time and age when I felt I was invulnerable to punishment humbled me dramatically. From that time on, I never made another comment or committed another deed that warranted physical punishment. It had taken me fourteen years of unregulated impulse control and forgetfulness, but this final act of rebellion and its consequence ensured that I would never do anything else to cause me to experience the wrath of Mom.

Smackdowns

Fighting was never one of my strong suits, although by the first grade I had one noteworthy victory to my credit. It wasn't much of a fight between Alvin Yancey and me, but what transpired afterwards compensated for the lack of drama that occurred when I bested him in the sandbox at recess. I don't believe we exchanged any blows in our confrontation; rather, I had pinned him down when the safety patrol boys intervened.

Both of us attended the same first-grade class taught by the feared and respected Ms. Cobbins. When the safety patrol brought in the whimpering Alvin, he said, "Two boys beat me up." Sympathetically, Ms. Cobbins said, "They did? Bring in the two boys."

When the safety patrol escorted me through the door, Ms. Cobbins said, "That's only one boy. Where is the other?" "That's him," Alvin said. "That's Two Boys." Realizing how he was mispronouncing my name, Ms. Cobbins let out a chuckle and allowed us to make peace. Alvin and I remained friends throughout our elementary school day without so much as a single altercation.

Within the next year or two I was exposed to the gentle art of boxing, a sport that required me to purposely hurt someone without provocation. Most of my boyhood confrontations had consisted of wrestling or shoulder punching that lasted until someone yielded. But as an eight-year-old, I, along with other boys from the neighborhood, gathered in the Field with two pairs of boxing gloves that I believe belonged to Allen "Gaulie" Wright.

As one of the youngest boys, I was asked to don the gloves and spar with Rand in a preliminary bout. Eagerly I put on the gloves to get my first experience at looking like Joe Louis. Rand put on the other pair. Here I was facing my friend, whom I didn't want to hurt, so I punched him on the arm. He responded by punching me in the face. I couldn't bring myself to hit him in the face, even with the encouragement of my "corner men." So I hit him on the arm again, and he punched me in the face. "Hit him in the face," my coaches told me. But the best I did was to hit his gloves as he held his guard up, causing a slight chain reaction, leading to his hitting himself in the face. Meanwhile, my face took a pounding until I felt something warm flow out of my nose before realizing that Rand had bloodied my nose.

The fight was stopped to allow me to run home with my head held high to minimize blood flow. As I trotted home, I could hear the cheers of victory while I realized that boxing was not for me.

The most baffling confrontation I encountered came at the expense of a younger boy who lived about two houses down from the dewberry patch on McIvor Street. One day a group of older girls, including Daisy Scott and Catherine Anderson, had gathered on the street in front of the Scott home. The boy, Gary, was about seven, while I was about nine, giving me a natural advantage in physical development.

Playfully, Cat threw a wood chip that hit Gary but caused no harm or pain. Gary accused me of hitting him with a rock, which I denied. He began to argue, saying he knew I had thrown the rock, and my words failed to convince him otherwise. When Cat confessed, even showing him the missile that had hit him, he disregarded her admission, choosing to focus his attention on me.

Then he decided to swing at me, which I avoided, warning him that he could not beat me. He swung again, but I blocked his lick and hit him on the shoulder. I smiled at his failed attempts to try to hit me, which frustrated him. Soon a stream of tears flowed down his face as he realized he was no match for me.

Through the tears he spied a rock that he made a move to grab. Before he could seize it, I grabbed him from behind and held him. He cried and demanded that I let him go. I told him that not until he promised not to try to fight anymore would I release him. He struggled but could not break my grip. After he settled down, I released him. He threatened to hit me with another rock, but after I called his bluff, he retreated and headed home. All of us who witnessed his behavior couldn't figure out why he was so determined to pick a fight with me, when he knew he was overmatched.

I never got an opportunity to solve the riddle of his behavior because he moved away before I ever saw him again.

My reluctance to hurt others gave me a decided disadvantage when, at ten years of age, I was involved in a series of three fights with Fred Smith. I have no clue what precipitated the first fight, but it started from some altercation we had in front of the white Carl Miller's house. Bill, Rand, Junie, Fred, and I were coming from some event near the end of the day when Fred challenged me to a fight.

Though I did not want to fight, I put up my dukes to defend myself. Before I knew it, Fred had slapped me in the face. The sting of being hit shocked me, but I was not angered by the blow. I still refused to try to retaliate in the same manner, causing me to receive a few more blows before the fight ended. Fred distanced himself from the group as they questioned me about my fighting strategies. I insisted that I didn't want to hit him in the face.

The thought of hitting Fred in the face caused me to fear facing him in the future because the consequences might be the same. Before the summer was out, Fred again challenged me in front of Bill. This time, near dusk, we squared off on the edge of McKinley Street across from Mr. Warren's house, when suddenly and uncharacteristically I tagged him in the jaw. Immediately I said, "I'm sorry, Fred." Shocked and defeated, he rubbed his jaw and went home.

I felt troubled by my action when I arrived at my house. After thinking about what I had done, I asked myself, "What do I have to apologize for?" He was going to hit me, but I beat him to the punch. I had hit him in the face, just like he had done me in the first fight. Now we were even. The more I thought about my victory, the more I wished that the friends who had witnessed my defeat could have seen the outcome of our second confrontation.

The summer was not over, leaving time for the rubber match. All that was needed was a reason, which I accidentally provided. A large group of us were preparing to play touch football on the Field by cleaning off some of the debris. I picked up a rusty can top and flung it off the Field. The wind blew the top toward Fred. The top grazed his elbow, and he asked who threw it. All witnesses pointed fingers at me as I tried to plead with Fred that this was an accident.

He approached me with fire in his eyes, so I knew we would have to do battle again. He swung at me, and I blocked the blow, countering with a lick of my own. To the delight of the other boys, the fight was on. The boys divided into two camps; one coached Fred, and the other coached me. I didn't want to take this fight any further, but I had to stand my ground.

Tucker, my main coach, pointed out Fred's weaknesses. "Every time he swings, he closes his eyes," Tucker told me. "The next time he throws a blow, I want you to go up under him and tackle him to the ground. Then you can pound the daylights out of him."

"But I don't want to do that. I don't want to hit him in the face," I insisted. Up to this point, neither Fred nor I had landed any other blows since my initial contact, which was fine with me. The other guys, however, wanted to see some action. I was reluctant to be their entertainment, but I did give Tucker some satisfaction by following part of his instruction. As Fred swung with his eyes closed, I tackled him to the ground, only to quickly get up without delivering the coup de grace.

"You had him. Why didn't you hit him when you had him down?" said a disappointed Tucker. I reiterated, "He's my friend. I don't want to hurt him."

I looked around at the crowd of guys, wondering why one of the older ones hadn't tried to stop this fight. My only hope was to take matters in my own hands. After sparring for an interminable length of time with no blows to any parts of our body except our arms, I told the crowd that I had to go to the bathroom. I promised to return, but somehow, I think they knew their source of entertainment was leaving them.

As promised, I did go to the bathroom, where I sat on the toilet with the door shut, saying to myself, "I'm going to sit here until I think they have all gone, then I'm just going to stay inside." Once I left the bathroom, I went to our front room and looked out the window at the Field, now vacant. I felt relieved that I had stopped the fight and cared little about what the crowd thought. They weren't fighting; I was.

The next day I saw some of the guys, who told me that they figured I wouldn't come back. No one actually blamed or taunted me. But I still had Fred to contend with. The next time I saw him, I asked him why he liked to fight so much. He had no memorable explanation, but for a long time, every time I saw Fred, I felt intimidated and afraid that I would have to fight him, doing something I hated to do: hurt a friend. Fortunately, we never fought again. As our paths crossed throughout his shortened life, we established a bond that lasted until his death.

School of Soft Knocks

Whenever an adult would ask me what I wanted to be when I grew up, I answered, "A doctor." I had no driving ambition to be a doctor; rather, it was one of six occupations listed in the childhood jingle that included "a butcher, a baker, a candlestick maker; doctor, lawyer, Indian chief." Of the six, being a doctor was more palatable than the other choices. As I prepared to attend Yoder School, my career choice accompanied me only as a means to curtail conversation.

The thought of going to kindergarten thrilled me. Because my birthday was in October, I received my first educational setback: having to wait out almost an entire year before enrolling. The upside of this setback was that I would be attending school with two of my best friends, Rowena and Junie. Since kindergarten was not mandatory, we missed accompanying Ersie McCoy and Rand, both of whom started school in the first grade.

Our move to McKinley Street coincided with my first year of attending Yoder School. Kindergarten brought me in contact with some of my former friends, Thomas Crews and Lillian Roane, both of whom were twenty days older than I was, thus under the same grade restriction.

Kindergarten was relegated to the basement of the school. A kitchen area separated our class from the third-grade classroom of Miss Goldsboro, who would be the first teacher to confuse me by marrying and changing her name to Mrs. Meadows.

Yoder School was about six blocks from our houses, giving us time to bond further as we walked to our destination. One of the first things we noticed about school was the role of the safety patrol. They had the power to stand in the middle of the street and stop traffic. As a kindergartener, Junie thought that he could imitate the safety patrol one day as we crossed Federal Street at the corner of First. Rowena and I reached the other side in front of Cochran's Store, but Junie decided to stop in the middle of the street as a car came down Federal.

Forming a cross with his outstretched arms, Junie bravely and foolishly faced the oncoming car, which slowed down as it approached him. Junie ran toward us after experiencing success as an ersatz safety patrol. Bolstered by this accomplishment, he sought to repeat his performance. Another car came over the hill, and Junie took his stance in the street. This time, instead of slowing down, the car sped up. Junie, realizing that this could end badly, dashed to the safety of the sidewalk and ended his brief stint as safety patrol impersonator.

One of the most important lessons I learned in kindergarten started from my appreciation of the drawing skills of my brother Lafayette. Now a teenager, he drew me a picture of a two-story house that I showed to Mrs. Anderson. She commented on how nice a picture it was, then asked me a loaded question: "Did you draw this?"

As a five-year-old who wanted to please his teacher, I succumbed to the tone of suggestibility in her voice and said, "Yes." Then, as if she had set a trap, she softly asked, "Could you draw me another one?" I looked at the house and thought, "I can do this. The house is made of straight lines. All I have to do is draw what I see."

Mrs. Anderson gave me a sheet of paper and a pencil, leaving me to prove my artistic skill. When I drew the first line that was supposed to be the side of the house, I knew I was in trouble. My level of hand and eye coordination was not remotely close to Lafayette's. I erased the line, smudging my paper and wondering how I could get out of this predicament.

I toiled at reproducing the house, but when I finally finished, my house looked like it was falling down. While I agonized at being exposed, Mrs. Anderson attended to her other kindergarten students. I showed her my crude drawing full of smudge marks, saying I messed up. She gave me another sheet of paper and suggested that I try again. Mercifully, she never asked to see my sad little picture. She must have realized that I had suffered enough and wanted to leave me with some self-esteem. One thing for sure was that I would never again take credit for someone else's work.

By the time I entered the first grade, Ms. Cobbins' reputation had achieved legendary status. She was considered a tough disciplinarian. Her voice bellowed, striking fear in the hearts of first-graders.

One of the first tasks we had in her class was to write our names. When I spelled DuBois using a capital "B," she scolded me, saying it should be a small "b." Too cowardly to argue, I complied with her demand but told Momma about the incident when I got home. When I went to school the

Lillian Roane, Densimore Evans, and my sister Billie share a pose at our 1955 May Day celebration at Yoder School.

next day, the matter had been resolved, and I felt happy and relieved to be able to spell my name correctly.

In one of our first classes, Ms. Cobbins had a word chart that she pointed to, listening for our responses. For the first few words, I blurted out the correct answer before the rest of the class. Ms. Cobbins took note of this and rewarded me by having me to come up to her desk and sit beside her while she continued the word drill.

I remember her saying, "He's going to be somebody." Who, I didn't have a clue. I just reveled in being singled out to sit in the big blond oak chair, dangling my feet several inches from the floor. My ego leveled out, though, when Ms. Cobbins pointed to a word I didn't recognize and other students chimed in with the correct answer. Yet I felt good about being in school because I could do the work. I wanted to go every day.

In kindergarten, I had missed a day of school, so I set a goal of perfect attendance in the first grade. Then one Friday I woke up with a fever, making me too weak to go to school. I tried to convince Momma that I was well enough to go, but when she took my temperature, she decided otherwise. I pleaded that I would be better, but she insisted. Knowing I would miss school, I fell back into the bed and cried.

My crying, however, resulted not so much from wanting to go to school, but from what I knew would be a consequence of missing school. Friday was movie day. The Harrison Theater, in addition to showing regular features on Fridays, also showed the fifteen-minute serials that we called "the chapter pictures." This particular Friday was the final episode of *Superman Meets the Mole People*, and I had seen all the previous episodes. Now my hope of seeing the conclusion would be dashed by Momma's rule: "If you can't go to school, you can't go to the movies." So I cried not because of an insatiable appetite for learning, but for love of the silver screen.

By the time school let out that day, my fever was gone, and I was healthy enough to resume my normal activities. But rules are rules, so I had to depend on Billie to describe the outcome of the movie while I stayed at home playing alone and listening to the radio. My absence that Friday, though, would mark the last time I would miss school throughout my elementary and high school days.

An overflow of second-grade students caused me to be separated from my close friends and to bond with new ones. As part of the overflow, a select group of us wound up in a small classroom sandwiched between the regular-sized classrooms on the second floor. Mrs. Byrd, our teacher, had the luxury of a small group of students to whom she could pay more attention. I longed to be with my Junie and Rowena but learned to adapt.

One of my Christmas presents in 1951 was a small chalkboard with the cursive alphabet painted above the slate panel. I practiced forming the letters so that by the time I entered second grade, I felt myself to have an advanced skill. I discovered, though, that Janet Medley and several others also could write in cursive, making my accomplishment less exclusive than I had envisioned.

The most memorable person in this class was Robert "Sonny" Tanner, part of the extended Tanner clan that included Phil, Polly, Jerry, and Bobby. One day during the music segment of our class, Mrs. Byrd instructed us to get out our music books and turn to the song "Happy Little Johnny."

We all had solo opportunities to sing the selection, but when Sonny sang, his melodic voice was better than everyone else's. I followed each word and note as he sang and realized that he had a future in music far beyond the average second-grader. Mrs. Byrd showed keen interest in his voice and seemed to be as mesmerized as the ancients who had heard the mythical, musical Virgil charm both man and beast. Sonny would eventually embark on a career that involved singing and playing drums with the Jivers, one of the most popular rhythm-and-blues bands in Lynchburg. He would also teach himself to play several instruments, including keyboards and trumpet.

Third grade united me with my close friends Rowena, Junie, Lillian, and Thomas. I was happy to have as my teacher Ms. Ruth E. Jones, who would also serve as my fourth-grade teacher.

Fourth grade brought me in contact with several students who shared class with their kin: James Turpin and his older brother, Harry, who, with their younger siblings Pauline, John, Earl, and Randolph, lived next door to Aunt Pearl on Second Street; LeVerne Jenkins and his sister, Bernice, who rode the bus from Rivermont; Theodore Austin, who was in class with his aunt, Delores, although he was older than she; and, from Harrison Street, George and Steve Rucker.

George had to wear a clunky neck and chin brace, which he detested. It was designed to straighten his curved spine but limited his ability to play normally. He often shed this contraption so he could participate in playing football and all of the other physical activities in which young boys engaged.

I also reunited with Teeny Hopkins, who had transferred to Yoder School. We renewed our friendship, but somehow, a misinformed student, Betty Jean Ferguson, relayed a message to me that Teeny had said she was my girlfriend. Though this would have been a puppy-love coup, Teeny insisted that she had been misquoted, saying that I was an old friend of hers. That statement relieved some boy-girl angst, though it would have been nice to have a girl as pretty as she was to be a girlfriend.

One of my most intriguing and mysterious classmates was Delores "Dot" Cobbs, who lived on Fifth Street. Absenteeism plagued her, causing her to miss school for weeks at a time. When she did come to school, it was as if she had been there all along, because she was never behind on her lessons. She would tell me that she stayed out because she was sick, but I always thought there was something deeper. I felt that Ms. Jones held the key to her absenteeism, though I had no evidence to back up my speculations.

Delores was one of the brightest girls in our class but seemed to have the weight of the world on her shoulders. Her homely features added to her demeanor, though I considered her a true friend as well as classmate. She would transfer to Robert S. Payne but would never have a chance to blossom. If ever there was a person who fit the profile of Langston Hughes's "raisin in the sun," it was Delores. She would drop out of school and die a violent death before she turned thirty.

My quiet demeanor and soft voice placed me in the good graces of Ms. Jones, who also had some concern that my hearing might be affecting my ability to speak at a normal volume. Her concern peaked when she challenged me to scream in my loudest voice in front of the whole third-grade class. The opportunity to scream unrestricted was the chance of a lifetime. I geared up to produce the most bloodcurdling Fay Wray scream ever heard in Yoder School. I inhaled deeply, ratcheted up my vocal cords two octaves above normal, and, with visions of shattering windowpanes, let out not a sound. Nothing but a wisp of air passed from my mouth. My classmates snickered at my failed attempt, while I suffered the embarrassment reserved for a Charlie Brown moment.

After settling the class down, Ms. Jones gave me a chance for redemption. I gathered myself, more determined than ever to make my mark in vocal history. I sucked up enough air to cause a vacuum in the room and then let out a second deafening silence. This repeat of my first attempt, another abysmal failure, added to my growing portfolio of youthful gaffes.

Ms. Jones took note of my strained silence and contacted Momma, recommending that she take me to the Health Department to get me tested for hearing problems. I tried to explain why I had failed to scream, but Momma followed through with Ms. Jones's suggestion and escorted me downtown.

When we arrived, the white female audiologist subjected me to routine tests that revealed nothing significant. Then she selected a book on my grade level and prompted me to read aloud. I amazed her by reading fluently. In fact, she was so fascinated by this young black boy's being able to read that she listened as though I were a musical prodigy. Reveling in this unaccustomed attention, I fell into my reading groove and was about to impress her further when misfortune disrupted my moment in the sun.

I had charmed her with my reading skills, words had flowed effortlessly from my mouth, and then a hair or some small foreign object eased down my throat, paralyzing my speech. Valiantly, I tried to force words from my throat, but received no cooperation from my vocal cords. A dry, rasping whisper replaced the words that had established a mood of awe only moments before. Tears of discomfort welled in my eyes as I strained in vain to master my vocal demons.

Eager to assist me, while puzzled at this occurrence, the audiologist accompanied me to the water fountain, asking, "Does this happen often?" Frustrated by the turn of events, I lied and said, "Only when I read a lot." After gulping down the water, I was ready to resume demonstrating my reading prowess. Unfortunately, the spell had worn off, and she said further reading was unnecessary. I do believe, though, that I had erased a stereotype about poor black children not being able to perform academically as well as whites.

My memory problems created an awkward situation with one of my classmates. While walking down the aisle of our class, I picked up a pencil/ink eraser that I thought I had dropped. Gloria Lacy, who was bussed from Rivermont along with several other students, told Ms. Jones that I had taken her eraser.

Ms. Jones asked me to hand over the eraser, which I told her I had brought from home. After listening to my weak claims and Gloria's seemingly airtight case, she examined the eraser and asked me to explain how it got the initials "G.L." At a loss to think of any explanation except "Good Luck," which I was assuredly not going to utter, I conceded defeat.

Ms. Jones told me to apologize, which I did, still trying to figure out how my eraser had morphed into Gloria's.

My answer came when I went home and found my eraser, identical to hers sans initials, and then realized what I had done: I had transferred the knowledge of having the eraser into a false reality of having hers. I now had to come to grips with the lies I generated when confronted with the truth. Learning that what I thought I remembered did not comport with actual events was a bitter pill to swallow.

The only time our school had to be evacuated was one October, just prior to my tenth birthday, when Hurricane Hazel roared into town. The strength and direction of the storm were still in doubt when we arrived at school, but as its intensity increased, parents were called to pick children up. Since our family didn't have a car, I prepared to walk home.

Fortunately, Rowena's father arrived and allowed me to ride home with them. This act of kindness I never forgot, and it showed the cohesiveness of our neighborhood. I was extra happy for the ride because the shoes I was wearing had cardboard in them to cover holes in the soles. I never disclosed this humbling aspect of our poverty; rather, I was happy to be in the company of my close friend.

Near the end of fourth grade, the designation of having an overactive mind came to pass. Although I was getting mainly A's and B's in all my subjects, with the exception of C's in my unstable handwriting, something was about to change.

On one of my last weekly arithmetic tests I got the shock of my educational life when I received a grade of forty. It was not that I didn't know the work, but my mind and my brain had worked in two different time zones. Ms. Jones accused me of being careless, which I accepted after reviewing my series of simple mistakes. Yet I couldn't recall writing down some of the answers on my paper. I felt like a mental gap had wedged itself between my test paper and my abilities. Had I been living in the era of special education, I probably would have been red-flagged, assigned a label, and given an IEP (Individual Educational Plan).

In September of 1955, new faces popped up in Ms. Hill's fifth-grade classroom. Robert Rucker joined his two brothers, while Fred and Gloria Smith became the brother-and-sister team to replace LeVerne and Bernice, who had transferred to Armstrong Elementary. Warren Canada, our newspaper deliverer, also joined our class. Warren and I had a short-lived ritual when he delivered our morning paper. We would throw rocks at each other, but his aim was truer than mine, causing me to get hit, while my errant missiles never exacted revenge. He would transfer to Payne School before the end of the year.

Robert Rucker laid the foundation for the transition in Junie's nickname. Saying that Junie's hair looked like a shack, Robert began calling him "Shack." Over the years this nickname morphed into "Shag," and until his death in 1999, that was the name most people called him. Just as I never could bring myself to call Rand "Hunt," I would never call Junie by any other nickname.

My failing test grade at the end of fourth grade was an ominous sign of what I would face in fifth grade. Now that my handwriting had improved, I had set a goal of getting all A's in at least one grading period; however, math and my wandering mind held in check any effort to fulfill my quest.

Each Friday was my doomsday in math. Although I had few problems during the week, math tests on this fateful day caused me grief, consternation, and insecurity. Getting failing grades in math tormented me, especially when Ms. Hill returned my grades and I could instantly spot my simple mistakes. I remember Rand saying, "You may get good grades in spelling, but I get better grades in math."

No matter how much I reviewed my answers before submitting my tests, I managed to bypass the obvious. On one test, either Ms. Hill overlooked my incorrect answers or, out of sympathy, gave me a passing grade. Louis Coles, another bright student, was suspicious of my getting a passing grade and asked to see my paper. By this time, I could see that a couple of my answers were wrong, and it was only through his insistence that I allowed him to see my paper. He compared our answers, pointing out my errors.

Though I wanted to have a passing grade, I took my paper back to Ms. Hill, where she sadly assigned me a failing grade, much to the delight of Louis. Throughout the fifth grade, seldom did I manage to pass our weekly test. Ms. Hill showed compassion by giving me C's on my report card, for she knew I was capable of doing the work. I wanted this ordeal to end and hoped it would not carry over to sixth grade.

Before I passed to this grade, Junie would again cause me to get into mischief. Like any ten- and eleven-year-olds, we leaned toward grossness. Our repertoire of immature behavior included creating a host of flatulent sounds by blowing on our arms. We timed our blowing so that Ms. Hill could not determine the direction of our noises. She addressed the class, stating that someone in the class was making animal noises. Junie and I snickered at her choice of words. She never was able to pinpoint us as the perpetrators, but she got some revenge when, while teaching the parts of speech, she caught Junie and me trading licks. In the midst of her definition of a verb, she marched back to us and slapped both of us on the shoulders, saying, "Hit. That's an example of a verb because it shows action." Both of us sheepishly paid attention from that point on, since we had been made examples in an embarrassing teachable moment.

Mr. Martin was the only male teacher in Yoder School, and I couldn't wait to get to his class, although I had some trepidation about math testing. Somehow the bane of failing Friday math tests dissipated, and I was back to my former self. During one of our weekly math tests, I felt my confidence had peaked enough to believe I had made one hundred on a test. Mr. Martin, sensing that some of us had done well on this particular test, baited us with a proposal.

"How many of you think you made one hundred on this test?" he asked. A few of us raised our hands. "If you are confident you made a hundred, then I'm going to offer you this deal," he continued. "I will grade your paper, and if anyone who said they believed they made a hundred gets one, then I will give you an extra one. But if I find any mistake on your paper, you will get half the grade you earn. Now how many of you think you made a hundred?"

Only two hands went up, Louis Coles's and mine. Mr. Martin scrutinized Louis' paper, and, finding no errors, rewarded him with the bonus score. When he got to my paper, he examined it with the same intensity. My confidence soared as I saw the red checks he put by each of my correct answers. At the tenth and final question, the thought of having an extra hundred settled in my head. Then it happened.

Mr. Martin discovered that I had forgotten to label my final answer. Even though my computations were correct, I had left off "gallon" to identify my last quantity. For that he deducted one point, leaving me with a ninety-nine. He divided the grade in half, as agreed, and I wound up with a forty-nine. Though I had received a failing grade, which was not the lowest one of the day, my ability to focus and do math had been restored. This grade was less of a shock than those failing ones I had received in the fourth and fifth grades, and my overall average for this grading period was still high enough for me to garner a B on my report card.

Sixth grade was the last grade in which I would receive corporal punishment. Mr. Martin was called out of his class to meet with the principal, Mrs. Lewis, and in typical sixth-grade fashion, we unsupervised children took advantage of his absence. The girls began chattering, while the more kinetic boys began throwing balled-up paper and chalk across the room. Soon erasers became part of the arsenal of missiles, and one errant eraser that I threw cracked a window.

Immediately, things got quiet except for some of the girls saying, "Aww, I'm gonna tell." Because of the bedlam, no one could identify me as the culprit, and I certainly was not going to rat myself out. When Mr. Martin returned, the girls, almost in unison, relayed the news to him.

The girls identified six boys, including me, as the missile-slinging culprits. Mr. Martin commanded us to march down to the front row seats of the bolted-down desks. We sat on the row like prisoners awaiting the firing squad. Mr. Martin took out a thick yardstick and doled out a single whack to our thighs as we sat.

Compared to the sting of the switches Momma wielded, the sting that the yardstick produced was a piece of cake. I endured my punishment, fearing the worst if Momma ever found out what happened. Fortunately, Mr. Martin kept this incident in-house, and my flesh was spared. Since Mr. Martin could no longer trust us to act responsibly, he would get a seventh-grader from Ms. Anderson's class to monitor us whenever he had to leave his room.

No matter how hard I tried to get all A's on my report card, I usually fell short in either social studies or math. In one six-week period, all my grades pointed towards perfection. I had balanced my studying in such a way that I was assured of reaching my goal. But once again, fate had other plans. A week before the end of this six-week cycle, Mr. Martin got sick, and we had a substitute, George Williams, who lived in the duplex mentioned in my escape from the white boys.

Although my grades were A's, George (as we called him outside of class) gave me a B in social studies and a B in spelling. My eager anticipation turned to disappointment. When confronted, George said everybody got the same grade they had received the prior six weeks. When Mr. Martin returned, the grades had been posted, and he was unable to change them. My zeal for getting all A's fizzled, though I felt good about eliminating C's from my report card.

Rowena McDaniel, age twelve, stands between her sister Sharon, on the left, and Lynette Colmore, who was staying with her mother, Delores, at Miss Elaine's house. Our four-room house is on the left.

Before I left the sixth grade, Mr. Martin had solidified my status as being economically poor. When asked a question about determining class status, he told us that if a family was making less than $3,200 a year, then it was designated as poor. I calculated and recalculated my family's income and could not get the numbers to add up beyond $2,600. I was officially poor in dollars, but because of my outlook on life, I felt rich in sense.

Ms. Frankie Anderson, my seventh-grade teacher, was by far the cornerstone of our school. No nonsense took place in her class as she prepared her students for the transition to legendary Dunbar High School. For some of the older students, one way or the other, this would be the last year they would attend Yoder School. For others, the excitement of being in high school fueled a desire to represent Yoder School with pride.

Our small class contained a nucleus of bright students who were as academically prepared as those in the monolithic Robert S. Payne Elementary School. Out of a class of twenty-two students, our shining stars included Rowena, Lillian Roane, Ellen Vaden, Louis Coles, and me. We added two precocious students to the mix when sixth-graders Linda Hubbard and Diane Johnson, Louis' sister, were promoted to the seventh grade after attending summer school sessions in order to skip a grade. We had other students with special skills and talents who I believed had the potential to excel, but they had other priorities besides the pursuit of excellence in academic education.

Now that I was in the seventh grade, I was at the top of Yoder's student hierarchy. I opted to become a safety patrol, not because I was civic-minded, but because of one of the perks associated with the duties: a trip to Washington, DC, to march in a parade down Constitution Avenue.

Ms. Anderson assigned me the corner of Second and Federal, which had limited student traffic. Though now I could officially stop traffic, I seldom asserted my authority. Most of the time I just stood around in my big sunshades, letting my mind wander. Sometimes I would get lost inside myself and fail to hear the bell ring. Then someone would have to call me from Second and Jackson to return to school.

Another duty I picked up was the selling of supplies to the other classrooms. Routinely, I went to each lower class with a box filled with pencils, paper, erasers, and other sundries that the school sold to students who had used up or lost these supplies. This duty gave me time out of class early in the morning, which I liked, but it also meant I would miss one of the daily math activities Ms. Anderson used to improve our grades. Each day she would give us a long calculation problem containing six-figured numbers. We either got a hundred or a zero on the problem. At the end of the week she would average the grade and it would then be factored into our regular grades. The outcome for me was more disastrous than beneficial, because computing long numbers gave my mind extra opportunities to wander. I would invariably mess up one or two problems a week, lowering my regular school grades instead of raising them. Other times I missed a problem because of my vendor duties. After a while, Ms. Anderson abandoned this practice, causing my grades to stabilize.

In preparation for high school, Ms. Anderson encouraged us to read books, which we logged on three-by-five note cards after completing a written book report. At first I approached this assignment with enthusiasm, but soon I found few books in our limited library that appealed to me and began padding my card with low-level books.

Ms. Anderson noted my lack of drive and told me I should be ashamed of adding fourth- and fifth-grade books to my collection. I felt somewhat awkward, but I was blinded by the ambition of having lots of books on my cards, because these cards were to accompany our records to high school. Before the end of the school year, I had accumulated three note cards full of book titles. Poetic justice came to me when I lost two of the cards, reducing my reading collection to reflect what was closer to the actual number I had read.

Before I went to the eighth grade, I had to endure a physical change reminiscent of a Franz Kafka character. In the summer of 1958, I awoke one morning to find that the nipples on my chest had enlarged overnight. Immediately, I thought of one of the seven warning signs of cancer: enlarged breasts.

I began thinking of a shortened lifespan and agonized over how to break the news to Momma. Eventually, I told her of my fate, showing her my telltale symptoms. She looked at my body, gave a chuckle, and explained that I was just going through puberty. I immediately felt a sigh of relief, though I but had never heard of enlarged nipples as a body change in boys.

Humiliation awaited, as my mother, finding amusement in my hormonal changes, broadcast to her friends what I thought was a very intimate and confidential discussion. This information trickled down to the son of one of these friends, who joked with me about the incident. Embarrassed that my personal life had leaked to the public, I resolved to keep any further intimate details about my life to myself.

Since no one else I knew had experienced this pubescent alteration, I now had another reason for self-consciousness to add to my list. To add insult to injury, Momma bought me three striped tee shirts that conformed to my body. In addition to these shirts, my wardrobe included two sheer seersucker shirts, all of which revealed my new growth.

I was about to enter the eighth grade with boobs larger than those of some of the prepubescent girls in my class. My humiliation level reached an all-time low as I had to endure stares from others who saw my physical change as a male anomaly. One day at lunch, one of my classmates, Helen, even went so far as to press her index finger on my nipple to see how it felt. Each day when I woke up, I had to face the reality that this slight change in my body was causing me to become more self-conscious than ever. Throughout high school, I slowly adjusted and accepted how I looked, realizing that there was nothing I or anyone else could do about it.

Eighth grade reduced my student status from veteran to neophyte. Having more than one teacher and remembering class schedules took some adjustment that I soon overcame. My homeroom teacher, Ms. Coleman, was new to Dunbar, as was our band teacher, Mr. Russell. New students from other schools expanded my friendships. New students also increased the challenge of dealing with personalities that put me in awkward situations.

Reuben "Butch" Parrish, one of our shorter students, coaxed me into wrestling matches in the back of our homeroom at the conclusion of the school day and before Ms. Coleman arrived to dismiss us. Although I possessed superior strength and skills, he challenged me only on days when I wore Noon's hand-me-down shoes, which had hard leather heels and soles that gained no traction on the tile floor. Without traction, I was unable to defend myself properly, and when other students saw us rumble, they assumed that he was taking advantage of me. He knew that under different circumstances the outcome would have been in my favor, so he never responded to my challenges when I wore tennis shoes.

Throughout all of this, I accepted the outcome of our face-offs and never regarded our bouts as anything but ego-affirming conquests for him. Because I knew my abilities, winning took second place to having him feel superior to someone my size.

My class schedule included Mrs. Ferguson, my English teacher, who taught me one of the most important skills in language: the art of listening. The most revealing activity to which she exposed me was listening to my voice on a tape recorder. Until I heard my voice replayed on tape, my perception of how I sounded was completely different from the high-pitched voice that came from that cursed machine. I was so shocked to hear my voice that I went into denial, wondering who was behind the conspiracy to manipulate my voice in such an unflattering manner. It would take only a few minutes to realize that what I heard was what I was. I had to accept that how I heard myself and how others heard me were diametrically opposed.

Mrs. Ferguson considered that I was a prime candidate to benefit from afternoon employment. She had a friend who needed the grass cut around the office building at Fifth and Jackson streets. Though I appreciated Mrs. Ferguson's gesture, I liked having my afternoons free to play with my friends. Out of courtesy, I agreed to cut the grass. A wall that kept the yard level as Jackson Street sloped toward Sixth Street supported the landscape. The yard was enclosed by a wrought-iron fence, which made me feel imprisoned as I sloppily mowed the grass. When I finished, the lady came out to inspect my handiwork. She pointed to the patches of grass I had missed and my lack of trimming around the fence, and she gave me a sickle to complete my work. I piddled around the yard, thinking, "She must have mistaken me for Booker T. Washington. I am not trying to impress her. I can make as much money as she is going to pay me by caddying."

After a perfunctory effort, I told her that yard work was not for me. She paid me my pittance, and I went home in relief. The next day, Mrs. Ferguson asked me about the job, but I think her friend probably told her of my incompetence. I felt no shame, because I didn't want the job in the first place. I'm sure my actions did little to build my reputation as a hard worker.

Mr. Waters, my social studies teacher, detected one of my most visible qualities. It also was one that my friends frequently quizzed me about: smiling. I felt comfortable with this expression and found it complemented my burgeoning wit. Mr. Waters went so far as to call me "Smiley" in his classroom. Having a nickname that had meaning gave me a sense of worth, and I liked it better than my birth nickname, "Dusie." I became at ease with my new nickname and did what most young people did: I inscribed it on top of my desk. This sobriquet was short-lived because except for Mr. Waters, nobody called me "Smiley." "Dusie" it was, and "Dusie" it would always be.

My other teachers included Mr. Russell, band teacher; Mr. Pinn, gym; Mrs. Seay, science; and Ms. Early, math teacher.

My first grading period provided me with the surprise of my academic life when I received a ninety-nine in English and a ninety-eight in math. Combined with my other not-so-stellar grades, these high ones put me on my first honor roll.

Making honor roll elevated my academic status, since I was the only male in my homeroom to do so. My academic distinction, though, contributed to a trauma that I would not overcome for almost ten years.

Dunbar High School held an annual spelling bee, pitting representatives from each homeroom and grade against each other. When the contest was announced, our homeroom narrowed down our representative to Alvin Yancey and me. Although I had more name recognition from my honor roll status, I felt that Alvin was equally skilled at spelling. The consensus of the class leaned toward me, and I felt that I would do our class proud in this contest.

Eager to flaunt my spelling prowess, I mentally prepared myself to do battle with upperclassmen, envisioning myself as David felling upper-class Goliaths as I ascended to the spelling throne. That was my perception; reality had a different outcome.

All of the contestants gathered on stage behind the curtains as the rest of the students filed in. The moderator encouraged us to relax, but I was

In 1960, when I was in ninth grade, Billie posed in her graduation gown in front of Ms. McIvor's house. Billie chose this site because the house presented a more photogenic background than ours. The plant on the left is the sapling of the ailanthus tree.

pumped up. As we sat in our chairs, the curtains opened, and I was suddenly face-to-face with the largest group of people I had ever encountered. By the time the curtains had moved out of sight, my mind had gone blank with fear. I had never been on stage before, except in the safety of numbers in band concerts. Even in elementary school I had never spoken more than two lines total in all my classes, and that was in the classroom, not on a stage.

Now, experiencing my first solo flight on stage, I was about to crash and burn. Not only was the shock of seeing five hundred faces traumatizing, it prevented outside sounds from penetrating my fragile brain. To make matters worse, I was the first person to be called front and center to display my spelling acumen.

Still reeling from the sea of teenage faces, I floated to the microphone, oblivious to anything except my need to retreat from the stage. When the moderator called my word, I heard only unintelligible syllables. Stalling for time to decode the sounds, I asked the moderator to use the word in a sentence. I heard neither the word nor the sentence uttered. With my mind a complete blank, I garbled out letters of the alphabet that I am sure had no connection to the word I was supposed to spell. I didn't care. I just wanted to get off that stage, promising myself that if I survived this ordeal, I would never get on a stage again.

I did manage to get off the stage and kept my vow. For my entire high school career, severe stage fright prevented me from standing in front of an audience unless it was in the safe confines of the high school band. I would be a senior in college before I had enough courage to face and overcome my stage-fright demons.

Ninth grade signaled a gradual downhill slide from my eighth-grade academic achievements. Although I made decent grades, I felt handcuffed in algebra, because a few students in our class kept up so much disruption that we failed to progress beyond signed numbers. In English, I held my own until our teacher warned us during our second grading period that unless we turned our English notebooks in on time, we would receive a failing grade. I had completed all my assignments, and my notebook was ready for submission until Louis Coles asked to use it to get his work in order. Reluctantly, I loaned him my notebook, though he promised to place it in my locker before the start of class.

When the bell rang for our second-period English class, I went to my locker, where the notebook was nowhere to be found. Panicky, I searched every nook and cranny of my locker with no luck. My only hope was to pray that Louis would bring it to class. When he arrived in class, I desperately asked him about the notebook. He said he had put it in my locker, but once the bell had rung, it was too late to go back to retrieve it. Our teacher asked for the notebooks, and not a single student had one ready. I pleaded for permission to return to my locker, but she flatly refused, and as a result I received a seventy-two, my first failing grade ever on a report card.

When it was announced that I did not make honor roll for that six-week cycle, some of my classmates were shocked, even more so when they found out that I had failed English. Even with the failing grade, I had an eighty-eight average, but the seventy-two kept me off the honor roll.

I swallowed my pride and lived with the reality of the harsh world of school. I could have accepted this fate more honorably if I had not learned that students in another of this teacher's classes found themselves in a similar situation two grading periods later but were given no penalty.

Thus was I introduced to the double standard of education that would accompany me throughout my high school days.

Although I was a good student, one of the top male students in our class was John Cardwell, Jr., who was also my Sunday School classmate. John hailed from one of the most politically active families in the black community. His father was the president of the local chapter of the NAACP, and his uncle, Glover, was a driving force behind civil rights activities.

I considered John my intellectual nemesis, though he had more resources at his disposal. I could not match his intellectual or physical output. He was taller and more self-assured, and he had more exposure to the outside world. Because of his stature, I felt compelled to try to outperform him, which I seldom did. When John transferred to a private school, he left an intellectual void and an excuse for me not to push myself. Without him, I was considered by some to be the top male student in our class, since my name was often on the honor roll in the ninth grade. I felt that my ascendancy to the male academic throne was tainted, and I was only there by default. Since John was not there to press me, I began to take less interest in fulfilling the responsibilities that accompanied my unheralded academic status.

Girls in my class were dominating the honor roll charts. A former kindergarten classmate named Shirley Jackson, Lillian Hale, Ella Coleman, and Elsie Johnson joined our juggernaut of honor roll students from Yoder: Lillian, Rowena, Linda, Ellen, and Diane. Ellen would move to Williamsburg, where, I was told, she continued to excel.

Science was one of my saving graces in ninth grade. I made grades decent enough that Mrs. Lewis asked me to participate in the Western District science and math conference. She had limited knowledge of the type of test I would have to take, so she supplied me with advanced books that I studied religiously. The problem was that she had given me biology books to study, but the test I took at the conference was general science. As a result, I did miserably on the test and failed to place or even get honorable mention.

I vowed that the next year I would be ready for the biology test, and indeed, I did well enough to win second-place honors among the black schools in our district. By then, though, I had moved from McKinley to Jackson Street, across from the house where my family first settled in the city.

My ninth grade year started with my lacking funds to pay the rental fees for my books; consequently, I had to depend upon the kindness of my more fortunate classmates to keep up with my lessons. One of the first persons to reach out to me by sharing her book was Veronica Saunders. From the day she first allowed me to use her book, we became friends. She invited me to her house on Loudon Street to dine with her family, and her mother and father became close friends with my mother.

During the tenth grade, my desire for excellence in education had begun a downhill slide. I had received a bitter taste of grading discrepancies. I was having trouble in Algebra II, and music and sports dominated my teenage brain. My earlier grades had been so high that I knew I could coast. My interest in reading books fizzled as television filled in the gaps of my social isolation. I dabbled in participating in school activities but became disheartened by the thought of sacrificing time and energy that I could put to use hanging with my friends or becoming addicted to television.

The Sound of Music

By the time I completed the fourth grade, Ms. Jones had acquainted her class with all of the instruments of the symphony orchestra. Junie and I would discuss the merits of these instruments and took particular delight in hearing the deep resonating sounds of the contrabassoon, which for us represented musical flatulence. One of the last items our teacher presented to us before we advanced to fifth grade was the opportunity to take music in the summer of 1955, under the direction of famed Dunbar High School marching band director David C. Moore.

Rowena selected the clarinet as the instrument to learn, while I debated with my family on what to play. Initially I considered drums, but since Billie was taking drum lessons already, Momma didn't want two drummers in the family. She suggested the saxophone, but I declined, saying that it had too many keys for me. I chose the trumpet instead.

In our first lesson, Mr. Moore, instead of giving trumpets to his fledgling students, gave us the horns' mouthpieces. He told us that unless we were able to produce the appropriate sound with the mouthpiece, we would not get the rest of the instrument. I felt confident that I could produce the desired sound on the first try. I wrapped my lips around the mouthpiece and blew into it as if blowing up a balloon, producing a sound no louder than the one that emanated from me when Ms. Jones asked me to scream.

I blew again, and the only sounds I heard came from other students who had mastered the first step and received their instruments. Engulfed in angst as I saw my peers selecting choice instruments, I finally pursed my lips and blew the sound of admission, giving me the right to claim one of the remaining horns.

Once I got accustomed to blurting out notes on my trumpet, I envisioned myself as Harry James, playing "Cherry Pink and Apple Blossom White." So did every other young trumpeter. Compared to me, though, guys like Bobby Jackson and Carl Hutcherson, Jr., played with the embouchure just one step below the professional level. No matter how hard I tried, my lips could produce only muddled notes that showed I had little if any potential as a musician.

When the summer session ended, Momma told me that if I wanted to continue to play music, she would buy me a trumpet. Though I had limited ability, I promised to make good on her investment if she bought me the instrument. Momma went down to L. Oppleman's and purchased a Holton trumpet for $129.50 on the installment plan.

Rowena and I took lessons together, but when we left to go home, we were often accompanied by one of the older boys, Lawrence Perkins, who lived on Jackson Street in the Black Bottom. "Perk" was somewhat of a bully, and I had a hard time dealing with him because I wouldn't put my foot down. He never challenged me physically, but almost every day when he, Rowena, and I left our music class, he asked me to let him play my trumpet. Usually he asked me when we had nearly reached the top of Polk Street hill between Seventh and Eighth streets, across from the Swain family on a wall just above the Doswells.

Besides delaying our daily trek, Perk made me uncomfortable with his blaring of random notes that I felt infringed upon the peace and quiet of the neighborhood. When I would refuse to give in to his demand to see my trumpet, he would respond, "I ain't gonna hurt it." I never doubted his word, which left me without a forceful comeback. He would also tell me that I could play his trombone as a trade-off, something I didn't want to do.

For a whole summer session, this became a ritual. I did take the liberty of blowing his trombone once or twice, just as a means of self-appeasement, but I was too self-conscious about playing in the open to continue this practice.

To my relief, Perk ended his music lessons, while I struggled to advance. My lack of talent and dexterity relegated me to playing third trumpet, while the more skilled students who had better-developed technique and mastery played first and second trumpet.

Mr. Moore was a patient teacher, but I was an impatient learner. I wanted to play but didn't want to practice. Consequently, I lumbered along in class, trying to make the most of Momma's investment.

In my first year with my new trumpet, our music class prepared for the annual concert. Mr. Moore said that in order to play, each trumpet player had to be able hit middle C on the scale. This was a basic note that I had had no problem playing up until this time. Every trumpet player before me hit middle C with ease, and when my time came, I experienced another humiliation reminiscent of my "scream" in the fourth grade.

Lack of confidence in playing music became an Achilles heel. I was one of the least proficient trumpet players, but I could play basic notes. When I blew into my trumpet, the piston in the middle valve had turned, restricting the flow of air. A muted sound squirted out of the bell of my instrument as the other trumpet players snickered. I tried again, with the same result.

Mr. Moore moved on down the line of trumpet players that included Albert Mallet, Frank Betts, and Ralph Boulware, Jr., all of whom would be my classmates. As my body flushed with embarrassment, I dismantled my horn, twisting and aligning pistons, hoping to atone for my failure. Finally, I got it right and redeemed myself by playing the qualifying note. Mr. Moore understood my dilemma and graciously acknowledged that I would be playing in the concert.

By the seventh grade, my musical abilities and knowledge had improved significantly, but when I compared myself to others, I knew music was not going to be a career choice. Even so, I would stay in my bedroom and listen to my favorite album, "Louis Armstrong Plays W. C. Handy," convincing myself that it was possible I could imitate "Satchmo." Each time I put on the scratchy vinyl of "The Saint Louis Blues," I had to readjust my ego. I could not play even the first note with anywhere near the crystal clarity I heard on our hi-fi. After many feeble attempts, I resigned myself to enjoying the music I had not the lips to play.

I thought my early exposure to music would give me the edge in accomplishing something Junie hadn't done. Since my sister had drumsticks that I dabbled with, I believed I could challenge Junie to a duel of rhythms. I took the drumsticks to his house, where I pounded out simple rhythms I thought to be too complicated for Junie to duplicate. He repeated my patterns without hesitation and drummed out one of his own. I tried to duplicate it without success. "This can't be right," I told myself. "These ain't his sticks. I'm supposed to do this better than him."

Again, I took the sticks and pounded what I thought was a complex beat. Junie repeated my rhythms as if they were no challenge. Then he beat another complicated rhythm I could not reproduce. To avoid further humiliation, I ended the challenge and took the drumsticks home. Junie had a talent I could not match. In fact, he would go on to master the drums, becoming an outstanding drummer for the Dunbar High School marching band.

Another ego-shattering musical experience also came from Junie, who told me he had been at the Ruckers on Harrison Street, where he had a chance to pluck out "Honky Tonk" on their guitar. Eager to see if I had the talent to repeat his success, I went over to their house and watched Steve, George, Robert, and Freddie take turns on their instruments. I watched their fingering; the song looked simple enough to play. When my time came to try, I got a glimpse at my uni-dimensional musical abilities. I discovered I could not do two different things at the same time. Thus any thought of being the next Jimmy Reed or Chuck Berry faded with notes that sounded like I was plucking rubber bands.

Mr. Moore conducted music lessons at Yoder School in my former second-grade classroom. Lillian, Rowena, and Ellen played clarinet proficiently, while I limped along with my trumpet. Though I had no particular ear for music, I was able to learn musical signs and symbols and could read music if it wasn't too complicated.

One of the last activities Mr. Moore conducted with us was an oral test with first-, second-, and third-place prizes. Although I knew many of the answers, he seemed to favor the girls, and Lillian, Rowena, and Ellen got first, second, and third places, respectively.

Ironically, this was the same order of a seventh-grade science project contest held by Ms. Anderson. We had to design scrapbooks with magazine pictures that showed different types of energy. I had spent a lot of time in collecting, organizing, and creating what my classmates thought would be a sure winner.

Ms. Anderson and Mrs. Lewis, the principal, judged our projects, and when it was over, I experienced another ego-deflating experience. I had reversed the "uo" in fluorescent in two of my captions, and, reminiscent of the math test in Mr. Martin's class, I received costly deductions that caused me to miss out on receiving a higher award than fourth place. Each of the girls got a small stipend for her efforts, while I received honorable mention, a penniless consolation.

I tried to attribute my error to Momma, who, when asked, couldn't confirm my spelling of "fluorescent." I also tried to use the excuse of being too poor to have a dictionary. Neither of these situations satisfied my need for a scapegoat. I knew that the reason I had failed to win was overconfidence and my unwillingness to go the extra mile in fact-checking.

Mr. Moore retired in 1958, at the end of my seventh-grade year. When I entered the eighth grade, I would have a new band teacher, Mr. Joseph L. Russell. Eighth-graders were classified as sub-freshmen, thereby keeping us from entering the ranks of full-fledged band members. We were the junior band without access to the purple and gold uniforms that the upperclassmen wore.

One of Mr. Russell's innovative approaches to showcase the junior band was to organize the community and parents around having us perform at football games. Since we didn't have uniforms, Mr. Russell requested that parents buy blue and white satin cloth and design capes that would be worn with black or blue pants and white shirts.

Momma had no problem designing my cape, which I wore with pride and trepidation, since it meant I would have to walk conspicuously through the streets in my uniform and carry my trumpet to school. Sensitive about being noticed, I tried to walk on the sidewalks that had the least amount of traffic. I felt more comfortable when I arrived at school, seeing my classmates attired as I was. There was safety in numbers.

Safety in numbers worked against me when, in the spring of 1959, I experienced an emotional setback. Our band had met at E. C. Glass High school to practice for commencement. At the end of practice, I went backstage to retrieve my trumpet case. Soon I found myself surrounded by a group of upperclassmen. When I bent down to pick up my case, one of them accused me of bumping into him and pushed me onto another older student. Before I could get my balance, he pushed me over to another, and pretty soon I was being bounced all over the place.

Though I wasn't physically hurt, I felt powerless to retaliate. Mostly I felt betrayed because among the group of boys was one I had considered a friend. The pain of seeing him conform to the group caused tears to stream from my eyes as I finally picked up my case, sniffling in defeat. When I exited from the side of the school stage, I ran into Rowena, who wanted to know what had happened. I was too upset to say anything and walked home alone with the echoes of taunts and laughter reverberating in my ears. I had to suck up my pride as I promised myself that I would never put myself in a situation where I would allow others to make me cry. I also promised myself that when I got older, I would never treat underclassmen the way I was treated.

At the beginning of ninth grade, Mr. Russell had an excessive number of trumpet players, so he asked me about switching horns. He introduced me to the baritone, the second largest brass instrument in the band. I welcomed the opportunity to try something new. Although the fingering of the instrument was the same as the trumpet, I had to learn how to read notes on the bass clef, since trumpets play treble clef notes. I had access to treble clef baritone music, but I wanted the challenge of learning how to read bass notes.

There was one baritone player, a senior named Archie Callahan, who took me under his wing. The biggest drawback to playing the baritone was its size. In order for me to develop a semblance of proficiency, I had to lug that instrument up and down the hills of Jackson or Polk streets until I got home. Carrying schoolbooks and the baritone slowed my journey, making me wish that I lived closer or could catch a ride. Neither happened.

Since I had an aversion to being noticed, I had to face the cognitive dissonance associated with being in the band. In order for me to get to the high school to play at our football games, I had to walk through the streets in full band regalia. Wearing the purple and gold uniform made me more conspicuous than I desired to be. Though I liked being in the band, I hated the thought of people watching me make the mile-long trek to Dunbar High School. Most of the time I met few people, though this did not decrease my self-consciousness or mitigate the thought of being singled out as a source of ridicule.

As my ninth-grade year came to a close, our band prepared for graduation activities. Archie was graduating, and, in true Hollywood fashion, exhorted me to take care of his instrument and carry on the legacy of baritone players. In atypical Hollywood fashion, I responded with indifference because I did not consider myself talented enough to care.

Final Days

By the summer of 1960, I had become the ranking teenager on McKinley Street, outside of Bill, who by now was making history by setting regional and state records in track, and Ronnie Douglas, who played on Dunbar's Western District championship basketball team. Each of them had traded playing on the Field for the better athletic grounds of Dunbar High School.

Junie and his family had moved to Dearington, while Paul and Morris seldom spent time on the hill anymore. Rand had found new friends, and Mitchell had left school altogether.

My choice of male friends from McKinley Street now included Reginald "Bud" Johnson, Wayne and Warren Scott, and the DeLoatch boys. All these playmates were several years younger, but I played with them without bias against their ages.

I knew it was time for me to make some adjustments to my play activities, though, when Ba'y Bro Patrick came up on our hill to deliver some wood and saw me wearing my cowboy gun and holster. Boys my age did not play cowboys and Indians, but on McKinley Street, I lived by a different set of rules. However, since I spent much of my time playing with peer-aged friends from the other streets named after presidents, I decided to hang up my pre-teen toys and focus on neighborhood sports so my reputation could escape tarnish.

As the years passed, the thrill of having electricity had been replaced by the dread of returning to 10 McKinley Street, a symbol of economic disparity. Even my classmate, Sheila Cherry, who was visiting Rowena one day, seemed shocked to see me in my yard, as I overheard her say, "Is that where DuBois lives?" Although we did not live in the worst house in the city, I was hard pressed to find many friends and classmates who could match the deplorable house in which we lived—the exception being the houses on the other part of McKinley Street.

To offset the poor quality of our house and in preparation for a better life, Momma stocked our house with quality furniture. She said that it was better to buy good furniture that would last than to buy inferior furniture that had to be frequently replaced.

Our fortunes were soon to change as Momma and Daddy, who had been house hunting, narrowed their search to two houses, one on Harrison Street in College Hill, and the other on Jackson Street a half-block from Yoder School. I felt a change of neighborhoods might give me a different perspective and a chance to broaden my friendships.

I did not know how close we were to moving until Momma called me upstairs and spread $1,500 in cash on her bed. "This is the down payment on our new home," she said. "We are going to be moving to 89 Jackson Street. We had thought about the house on Harrison Street, but we decided on this one." Although I wanted to make a complete change, moving anywhere with both plumbing and lights beat living as a semi-rural teenager.

The house at 89 Jackson stood out from others on the block because of the whitewashed cinder block wall bordering the small front yard and the screened-in front porch. Irony featured in my parents' selection of homes, because we were going to move across the street from the first house they had lived in when they relocated to Lynchburg from Bedford County. Our family was about to move in its fifth house in Lynchburg, and none had been farther than four-and-a-half blocks from the first one.

Although I had accumulated rich memories in my ten years on the Hill, I was painfully aware of the inadequacies of our four-room house. I looked forward to living in a house without shame. Our move happened while I was in school. I knew when I left Dunbar at 3:20 that warm September afternoon that my walk would be five blocks shorter.

When we moved, I wanted to obey the words of Lot, who told his family, "Do not look behind you." Once I left McKinley Street, I had no intention of going back. Momma tried to force my hand when she told me that we had left our trash can in the backyard. I had also left two highly prized Louisville Slugger baseball bats I had bought for our Little League team. Neither the prodding of Momma nor the loss of my cherished possessions could motivate me to take that four-and-a-half-block walk back to 10 McKinley Street. I couldn't see myself walking through the streets with a trashcan, so the bats would have to be collateral damage to my self-consciousness. Momma said I had too much pride, but it was more fear of the unknown that prevented me from using common sense. Even though I was moving only a short distance away, I separated myself from McKinley Street, the same way others did. I would not return until I graduated from college.

My brother Lafayette and Miss Elaine sit on her front porch in September of 2011.

Lafayette stands in front of 10 McKinley Street in 2003.

Epilogue

The landscape of my ten-year residency has gone through both subtle and dramatic changes. The part of McKinley Street where the Austins lived shows no sign that human activity ever took place there. A short driveway now used by the residents of 46 Federal is the only evidence of the former street. And among the houses demolished in the first block of Harrison Street were the homes of the Ruckers and the Wrights.

The first two blocks of Federal Street, descending from the Douglas home at 44 Federal to the Hawkins home at 24 Federal, have been renamed Hollins Mill Road. The Douglas home remains active, while Mr. Jesse's vacant home, still vacant, is property of the Lynchburg Redevelopment and Housing Authority. The double tenement house at 40 Federal has been razed, as have been three of the four houses in the first block of the former Federal Street, including the Anderson home. Only the Hawkins house, now boarded up, remains on this street.

The McBride billboard that hid the Scotts' home remains, but the house at 171 McIvor Street that once held the largest family in our neighborhood is no more. The DePriest house was razed before the Scotts' home. The McCoy house at 275 McIvor remains in the family, while the stately Isbell home at 474 McIvor at the end of the cul-de-sac has changed ownership, acquired by the Jones family, whose son, Herman, attended Dunbar High School with me. That house has also gone through renovations that have reduced the mystique it once held. A house has been built in the area where I collided with Mitchell as we rode our bikes, and the dewberry patch has died off, leaving a vacant lot as its legacy.

Blackwater Creek now features asphalt bike and nature trails that were once footpaths and railroad tracks. As part of the nature trail system, lights in the ceiling now illuminate the dark areas of the tunnel. The blackberries fell victim to the ubiquitous kudzu, but the city of Lynchburg got vengeance by destroying every vestige of the foreign invader in our blackberry domain. The only fruit that remains in the area is the patches of red raspberries near the now-hidden spring and near the entrance of the Blackwater Creek trail above the Hollins Mill dam.

On the hill of McKinley Street where I lived, the surprise of the community is that our former home, built in 1910, has endured for one hundred years. The DeLoatch home fell into disrepair and is now a vacant lot. The Warren house has been razed, and Ms. McIvor's home burned down. The McDaniel house has been remodeled and is occupied by Miss Elaine's daughter, Brenda. A one-story double duplex apartment has been built on the Field, and the view of Rivermont from the apex of McKinley Street is obstructed by verdant growth at the dead end. The dead end is also used as additional residential parking.

Miss Elaine is the most durable reminder of days gone by. At the time of this writing she is eighty-nine years old, though her face shows few wrinkles.

Our former house not only stands, but now features indoor plumbing. The side porch has been enclosed, and a deck has been added behind the kitchen. Instead of three fifty-five-gallon oil drums, an oil tank on the west side of the house provides fuel. Concrete has replaced the wood siding of the crawl space. Replacement windows have reduced the drafts of bitter winter wind, and asphalt tiles have replaced the tin roof.

Nick Willoughby and Katherine Grazier, a white couple, bought the house in 2004. I first met Nick while he was in front of his house discussing a sewage problem with city maintenance workers. He invited me into the house after I told him that I was writing a book about my life on McKinley Street. He showed me some of the other improvements to the house, including replacing the kitchen window with a door that leads to his deck. He plans to put vinyl siding on the house and rebuild the room that replaced the back porch. Nick said that deer and a variety of birds regularly pass through the yard.

Nick said he believes he lives in the best house in the city and that living in this house is like living in two worlds: he is in the urban world when he

goes out his front door, and he communes with nature when he goes out on
his deck. When he told me how he felt about living here, I knew that this
humble house had inspired in Nick the same feeling it had evoked in me
and that the spirit of 10 McKinley Street still lives.

Contrary to my earlier vow of refusing to revisit my former
neighborhood, I make a practice of returning to some part of it whenever I
am in town. Whether standing on the foundation of the former mill, where
the creak of the grinding wheels still echoes in my mind, or going up on
the hill to chat with Miss Elaine, I remain willingly, rather than reluctantly,
connected to the ten-year experience that shaped my life.

McKinley Street can now boast of two signs that were missing during my
childhood: a street sign and a dead end sign. Each symbolizes that life still
exists on this isolated street, but neither can capture the spirit that makes
McKinley Street a vibrant part of my life and soul.

About the Author

M. DuBois Miller was born in 1944 at 62 Polk Street in Lynchburg, Virginia, and graduated in 1963 from segregated Dunbar High School with the yearbook designation "brainiest boy." In 1968, after earning a B.A. in biology from Hampton Institute, he was drafted into the U.S. Army and served a tour in Vietnam.

Following his discharge from the Army, he worked as a medical technologist and substitute teacher before beginning a teaching and administrative career with the Virginia Department of Correctional Education. His thirty-two years of service with this agency included work as teacher and principal at the Powhatan and Haynesville Correctional Centers and a variety of roles at the Department's central office in Richmond, including assistant academic director, director of staff development, director of curriculum and instruction, and assistant superintendent of adult academic programs. In 1978 he earned the M.Ed. from Virginia Commonwealth University.

Since his retirement from the Department of Correctional Education, he has taught cognitive biology at the Beaumont, Bon Air, and Hanover Juvenile Correctional Centers. The author of *Cell Tales: Recollections of a Correctional Educator* (2009), he has been married to Shelia for more than thirty years and has two grown children, Edward and Adrienne, both of whom graduated from the University of Virginia.

References

Bell, Carolyn, ed. *Remembering Tinbridge Hill in Lynchburg, Virginia, 1920-1970.* 2011

Hill's Lynchburg City Directories: 1899, 1938, 1948, 1949, 1951, 1952, 1956.

Photo Credits

Nancy Marion collection: 114, 115, 116, 117, 118

DuBois Miller: iv, 1, 4, 5, 8, 14, 21, 24, 32, 36, 38, 39, 43, 54, 62, 66, 67, 68, 70, 72, 91, 109, 135, 142, 149, 165

Hilda Adams: 44

Index

A

Abie's Café 114, 117
Academy 111
Adams Motor Company 114, 119
Anderson, Catherine 32, 132
Anderson, Chris 3
Anderson, Frankie 146
Anderson, Gloria 32
Anderson, Ida 3
Anderson, James "Boodie" 3, 94, 97, 100, 102
Anderson, Mrs. 136
Anderson, Ms. 147
Anderson, Newman 3
Anderson, Rosetta 3
Anderson, Ruth 32
Anderson, Willie 32
Arlington County 42, 43
Armstrong Elementary School 127, 142
Armstrong, Louis 157
Aunt Pearl 139
Austin, Lillian "Lee" 23, *44*, 153, 158
Austin, Randolph "Rand" v, 23, *38*, 55, 57, 66, 67, 68, 70, 71, 87, 88, 97, 99, 106, 107, 126, 131, 132, 133, 135, 136, 143, 161
Austin, Theodore 139

B

Backwater Creek 65
Bar-B-Que Grill 114
Bedford Avenue 97
Bedford County 1, 28, 97, 100, 162
Belafonte, Harry 112
Bell, Alexander Graham 16
Bell, Carolyn iii, v
Berry, Chuck 158
Bethune Nursery School 6
Betts, Frank 157
Bibee's Supermarket 108
Big Island, VA 7
Black Bottom 53, 156

Blackwater Creek 22, 24, 25, 32, 37, 55, 67, 70, 71, 72, 73, 74, 75, 80, 166
Blackwater Street 41
Blankinship, Grafton iv
Blue Ridge Mountains 28
Bolling, Julia *vi*
Boodley Boo 99, 100
Boonsboro 99
Boonsboro Country Club 97
Boonsboro Road 97, 98, 100
Boulware, Ralph 114
Boulware, Ralph Jr. 157
Braxton A1 Transfer 114
Brimm, Dennis 4
Brimm, Ralph 4
Brimm, Roland 4
Brimm, Sookie Jane 4
Brimm, Wilton 4
Brooks brothers 107
Brooks, Sonny 62
Brown, Jimmy 82, 124
Bunyan, Paul 62
Burnette, Granville 94
Byrd, Mrs. 139

C

Callahan, Archie 160
Calloway, Willie 102
Canada, Warren 142
Cardwell, John Jr. 153
Carey Insurance & Real Estate 114
Carey, Lukengus 114
Carl B. Hutcherson Funeral Home 31
Cary Chevrolet 111, 119
Caul, Gracie 4
Caul, Leslie 4
Caul, McKinley "Boochie" 4
Chambers Street 79
Champ 47, *50*, 52
Champ II 48
Cherry Pink and Apple Blossom White 156
Cherry, Sheila 161
Chestnut Hill 86
Chicago White Sox 95

Chrysler 114
City Cab 114, 117
Clay Street 73
Cobbins, Ms. 131, 138
Cobbs, Delores "Dot" 140
Cochran, Mrs. 108
Cochran's store 17, 107, 108, 109, 136
Coleman, Ella 153
Coleman, Ms. 148, 149
Coleman, Preston 95
Cole, Nat "King" 28
Coles, Linwood 94, 95, 96
Coles, Louis 143, 144, 146, 152
Coles, Percy, Jr. 94, 95
Coles, Roger "Bones" 94, 95, 97, 100
College Hill 86, 162
Colmore, Delores 146
Colmore, Lynette 146
Community Funeral Home 114
Constitution Avenue 147
Cook, Bobby Reid 94
Court Street 73
crawfish 69
Crawford, Ida 4
Crews, Clarence "Buddy" 97
Crews, Edith 26
Crews, Reginald ("Roughhouse") 26
Crews, Ricky 26
Crews, Thomas 135, 139
Crowder, Edward 98, 99

D

Daniels Hill 67
Davis, Bobby 26
Davis, Carl 26
Davis, Florence 26
Davis, Helen 26
Davis, Jack 26
Dearington 75, 76, 78, 79, 81, 96, 110, 121, 161
DeLoatch 13
DeLoatch, Casper 44
DeLoatch, Elvis, Jr. 44

DeLoatch, Lloyd 44
DeLoatch, "Pappy" 15, 29, 46, 61, 89
DeLoatch, Phyllis 44
Dennis, Evelyn 5
Dennis, Kate 5
Dennis, Maggie 5
DePriest, Clara 33, 106
Diane 153
Dickerson Buick 58, 114
Diggs, Lewis 87
Douglas, Ronnie 15, 35, 161
Douglass Hotel 119
Drac 52, 53
Dr. Dictor 50, 51
DuBois, W.E.B. 1
Dunbar High School 95, 146, 148, 150, 155, 158, 160, 161, 162, 165, 169

E

Earl's Café 114, 117
Early, Ms. 150
E. C. Glass High school 159
Eighth Street 156
Einstein, Albert 121
Eleventh Street 73, 111
Elks Rest Home "Club" 118, 119
Esso 114
Eubanks, Albert 91, 102
Evans, Densimore *137*

F

Fats Domino 12
Featherstone, Edna 119
Federal Street 17, 21, 22, 23, 25, 26, 27, 32, 33, 51, 56, 81, 85, 88, 91, 106, 107, 110, 111, 113, 114, 120, 136, 147, 165
Fels, Lorenzo 114
Ferguson, Betty Jean 26, 140
Ferguson, Mrs. 149
Fifth Street 31, 51, 80, 81, 106, 111, 113, *114*, *115*, 117, *118*, 119, 120, 126, 140, 149
Fifth Street Baptist Church 3, 78, 118, *125*
First Street 106
Floyd Street 5

Fort Hill 111
Foundation, the 25
Fourth Street 86
Fox, Clifford iii, 3, 13, 26
Fox, Miss Lucy 3, *4*, 96
Fox, Paul 3, 26
Franklin Coal Company 118
Franklin, Mrs. 5

G

Garland Hill 23, 67
Garland Street 2, 4, 5, 17, 86
Gentry, Joyce 27
Gentry, Maxine 27
Gibson, Leander 114
Glenn's Barber Shop 114, 120
Goldsboro, Miss 135
Goodwyn, Henry 114
Grazier, Katherine 166
Greene's Barber Shop 114
Green, William Jr. 3, 79

H

Hale, Lillian 153
Hall, Castle 27
Hall, Glenda 27
Hall, Junie 27
Hall, Mildred Ann 27
Hall, Woodrow 27
Hampton Institute 4, 14
Harper's store 118
Harrison Street 23, 65, 66, 68, 92, 126, 139, 158, 162, 165
Harrison Theater 106, 111, 114, *116*, 119, 120, 126, 138
Hartman, Elwood "Skeeter" 102
Harvey, William "Bud" 102
Haskins' Barber Shop 119
Hayslett, Mr. 108, 109
Hayslett's Store 17, 103, 107, 108, 109
Herndon, James Ben 2, 94, 102
Herndon, Silas 2, 94
Hesse, Herman 37
Hill, Ms. 143
Holiday Sales 114
Hollins Mill 70

Hollins Mill dam 22, 69, 166
Hollins Mill Road 21, 22, 24, 25, 32, 41, 55, 68, 69, 72, 87, 97, 127, 165
Hollins Mill Road bridge 22
Hollins Street 2, 3, 21, 22, 75
Holmes family 3
Hopalong Cassidy 93
Hopkins, Annette 3
Hopkins, Garnet 3
Hopkins, Haywood "Shug" 4
Hopkins, Milton 3
Hopkins, Vashti 4
Hopkins, Yvonne "Teeny" 4, 140
Horseshoe Bend 72, 73, 74
Hoskins Pontiac 119
Hoyle-Halsey house 106
Hubbard, Linda 26, 146, 153
Hubbard, Mark 26
Hubbard, Mary 26
Hughes, George "Mr. Zeke" 4
Hughes, Langston 140
Hughes, Ruby 4
Hughes, Wheeler 4
Hughes, Wheeler "Wee Wee" 4, 94, 102
Hunting, Amanda 114
Hurricane Hazel 61, 142
Hutcherson, Carl Jr. 156
Hutcherson Funeral Home 114, *115*, 117

I

Isbell estate 25
Isis Theater 111

J

Jackson, Bobby 156
Jackson, George 114
Jackson, Shirley 153
Jackson Street 1, 53, 70, 87, 107, 114, 147, 149, 153, 156, 160, 162
Jackson, Thomas 32
James, Harry 156
James River 22, 65
Jefferson Park 124
Jefferson Park Pool 4, 64, 71, 75, 82

Jenkins, Bernice 139, 142
Jenkins, LeVerne 139, 142
Jim Crow 105
Jivers 139
Joe 123
Johnson, Brenda "Boo Boo"
    27
Johnson, Diane 146
Johnson, Dr. Eldorado 80
Johnson, Dr. Walter 118
Johnson, Elsie 153
Johnson, Mary "Bumpsie" 27
Johnson, Miss Elaine 15, 16,
    25, 26, 27, 29, 32, 41, 45,
    46, 52, 56, 64, 92, 164,
    166, 167
Johnson, Reginald "Bud" 27,
    42, 161
Jones, James "Gator" 78, 79
Jones Memorial Library
    29, 52
Jones, Ruth E. 139, 155
Juvenile and Domestic Rela-
    tions Court 113

K

Kafka, Franz 148
Kentucky Hotel 116
Kirby Street 81
Kirkland, Gary 42, 43, 132
Kirkland, Lucille 42

L

Lacy, Gloria 141
Lee, Canada 112
Legacy Museum of African
    American History v
L&H Music Co. 114
Lightning, Willie 23, 24
Lone Ranger 93
L. Oppleman's 156
Loudon Street 154
Lovingston 31
Lucado Street 67
Lynchburg iii, iv, v, 15, 16,
    21, 37, 41, 58, 72, 112,
    113, 121, 139, 162, 166,
    169
Lynchburg General Hospital
    3, 22, 37, 70, 73, 80, 108

Lynchburg Redevelopment
    and Housing
    Authority 165
Lynchburg Stadium 4

M

Mack's Smoke Shop 114
Maglie, Sal 94
Main Street 86, 111, 119,
    129
Mallet, Albert 157
Mantle, Mickey 94
Marion, Nancy iv
Martin, Mr. 121, 144, 145
Mary Bethune Nursery 5
May Day 137
Maynor, Dorothy 1
McBride 33, 165
McCoy, Carroll 33
McCoy, Ersie 33, 135
McCoy, Mitchell v, 33, 37,
    38, 88, 103, 161, 165
McCoy, Obediah 2
McCoy, Robert 33
McCoy, Rosamond 33
McDaniel, Rowena Lois 35,
    39, 42, 44, 135, 136, 139,
    146, 153, 155, 158, 159
McDaniel, Sharon 146
McDaniel, William "Bill" v,
    35, 37, 55, 57, 66, 67, 68,
    70, 71, 73, 74, 79, 87, 88,
    126, 133
McDemon, Ruby 114
McGraw, Mrs. 109, 110
McGraw's Store 109, 110
McIvor, Phoebe 29, 47, 124,
    125
McIvor Street 21, 25, 32,
    33, 37, 53, 56, 57, 63, 88,
    89, 97, 105, 107, 132,
    153, 165
McKinley Street v, 4, 7, 8,
    15, 20, 21, 22, 24, 27, 28,
    30, 31, 32, 35, 45, 46, 54,
    55, 56, 61, 85, 87, 93, 97,
    101, 133, 135, 161, 162,
    163, 164, 165, 166, 167
McWane's 99
Meadows, Mrs. 135
Medley, Janet 139

Menlo Park 13
Merritt, Starling 12
Midway Country Produce
    114
Miller, Carl 17, 35, 133
Miller, Carl, Jr., "Noon" vi,
    1, 36
Miller, Carl, Sr. vi
Miller, Frances vi
Miller, Lafayette "Cutchie"
    iii, v, vi, 1, 2, 11, 13, 14,
    36, 47, 93, 106, 136, 164
Miller Park 83
Miller Park Pool 82
Miller, Wilhelminia "Billie"
    vi, 1, 9, 16, 31, 32, 35, 40,
    41, 58, 59, 62, 124, 137,
    138, 151, 155
Millner's Department
    Store 30
Minnis, John 59
Mitchell's Store 100, 101
Modern Beauty Shop 114
Monroe Street 31, 86, 113,
    118, 119
Monticello 29
Moore, David C. 155, 157
Morris 161
Mullins, Moonie 82
Murphy, Audie 37
"My Blue Heaven" 12

N

NAACP 153
New Deal Works Progress
    Administration 6
New Era Barber Shop 114
New York 55
New York, Garden City 55
Ninth 129
Norfleet, James "Otis" 53,
    94, 96
Norfolk & Western 30
North Nineteenth Road 43
Norvell Street 22

O

Odd Fellows Hall 114
Order of Eastern Star
    Lodge 114
Otey Cab 114, 117

P

Paine, Hubert 47
Paramount Theater 111
Park Avenue 118
Parrish, Reuben "Butch" 149
Parrish's Snack Bar 114
Patrick, Clarence Ba'y Bro 2, 94, 100, 161
Patrick, Joyce 2
Patrick, Nancy 2
Patrick, Patricia 2
Peaks of Otter 28
Perkins, Lawrence 102, 156
Pettis, Kyle 114
Pettis Shoe Shop 114, 119
Philadelphia 41, 42
Phillips' Coffee Shop 17, 108, 109
Phillips, Mr. 103, 108
Pinn, Carl F. 76, 150
Pittman Plaza 113
Plummer, William "Billie Boy" 3
Polk Street 1, 2, 3, 4, 5, 17, 35, 58, 70, 80, 86, 117, 160
Pollard, Melvin 102
Powell, Louise 53
Powell, Sandra 53
Princess 50, 51, 52
Pulaski Street 76

Q

Quarles, Chili 95

R

railroad tunnel 30
Reed, Jimmy 158
Reid's Pharmacy 114, 119
Richardson, Carolyn 42
Richardson, Christine 42
Richardson, Dennis 42
Richardson, John D. 42
Rivermont 27, 41, 42, 55, 62, 71, 86, 139, 166
Rivermont Avenue 9, 36, 97, 98
Roadmaster 56
Roane, Lillian 135, 137, 139, 146
Roberts, Mrs. Inez 114

Robert S. Payne Elementary School 140, 146
Robeson, Paul 112
Rochester 112
Rollfast skates 86, 87
Rose family 3
Rose, Lafayette Silas "Stretch", Jr. 32
Rucker, Gail 44
Rucker, George "Champ" 92, 139, 158
Rucker, Hilda 44
Rucker, Larry 44
Rucker, Robert iii, 142, 143, 158
Rucker, Steve iii, 139, 158
Russell, Mr. 148, 160

S

Santa Claus 85, 89
Saunders, Veronica 154
Schewel's Furniture Store 11
Scott, Cecilia 39
Scott, Daisy 132
Scott family 15
Scott, Gloria 31
Scott, Helen 31, 148
Scott, Henrietta 31
Scott, Henry Elmo "Junie", Jr. v, 31, 34, 35, 55, 57, 66, 67, 68, 70, 71, 72, 76, 77, 78, 79, 80, 81, 86, 87, 88, 96, 97, 98, 100, 101, 103, 104, 105, 106, 107, 125, 126, 127, 129, 133, 135, 136, 139, 143, 144, 155, 157, 158, 161
Scott, Pamelia ("Daisy") 31
Scott, Rebecca ("Becky") 31
Scott, Sarah 31, 127
Scott, Theresa 31, 44
Scott, Warren 39, 161
Scott, Wayne 38, 39, 53, 161
Scott, Yvonne Bonet "Bonnie" 39, 40
Sear 112, 113
Seay, Mrs. 150
Second Street 4, 5, 86, 88, 91, 102, 111, 139, 147
Seventh Street 156
Shine 100, 101

Shitty Creek 75, 78, 79
Simon, Janie 30
Simon, Johnny Boy 31
Simon, Morris 31
Simon, Paul 161
Simon, Paul Jr. v, 31, 35, 37, 71, 87, 88, 89, 106, 107, 126
Simon, Paul, Sr. 31
Sixth Street 149
Skin Tom 23, 99
Skip 41
Smith, Fred 26, 133, 134, 142
Smith, Gloria Jean 26, 142
Smith, Laura 27
Smith, Lillian 27, 56
Smith, Marvin 95
S.O. Fisher's Sporting Goods Store 86
Southern Aid Life Insurance 114
Sportsman's Club 114, 119
Stengel, Casey 95
Stepin' Fetchit 112
Stevens, Lee 58, 102
Stevens, Rev. Harvey 125
St. Luke's Lodge 114
Strong, Hector 113, 127

T

Tanner, Bobby 139
Tanner, Jerry 139
Tanner, Phil 139
Tanner, Polly 139
Tanner, Robert "Sonny" 102, 139
Tate Springs Road 26, 37
Taylor Street 31
Teenage Canteen 80, 118
"The Saint Louis Blues" 157
Third Street 53, 58, 86
Thornhill, Clarence 30
Thornhill, Harriet 30
Thornhill, Herbert 30
Thornhill, Hubert 30
Thornhill, Tucker 30, 134
Tinbridge Hill iii, v, 22, 26, 27, 32, 58, 71, 85, 94, 97, 98, 101, 106
Tisdale, Ann 3

Tisdale, Donald 3
Tisdale, Lula 3
Traynham, Sterling "Dog"
    94
tree of heaven 23
Turpin, Earl 139
Turpin, Harry 139
Turpin, James 139
Turpin, John 139
Turpin & Jones Billiards 114
Turpin, Pauline 139
Turpin, Randolph 139
Tweedy, John 32

U

Union skates 85

V

Vaden, Ellen 146, 153, 158
Virginia 7, 54
Virginia, Gladys 54

W

Wade, Nannie 3
Wall, the 25
Ward, Jesse 25
Warner Theater 111
Washington, Booker T. 149
Washington, DC 1, 39, 43,
    44, 147
Washington, George 62
Waters, Mr. 150
Watson, Thomas 16
WBRG 12
West Lodge 114
White Rock Hill 86, 95
White, Thomas 77
Williamsburg 153
Williams, George 106, 145
Willoughby, Nick 166
Wilson Funeral Home *115*,
    119
Wilson's Store 5
Wimbush, Clara 114
WLVA 12
Womack, Mrs. 51
World War II 27, 37
Wray, Fay 140
Wright., Allen "Gaulie" 131
Wright, Anna 32
Wright, Gloria *44*
Wright, Hugh *44*

Wright, Jenny *32*
Wright, Richard 44

Y

Yancey, Alvin 131, 150
Yoder School 87, 91, 102,
    135, 137, 140, 144, 146,
    153, 158, 162